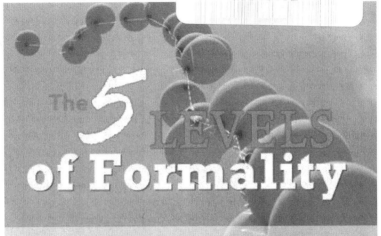

The 5 LEVELS of Formality

How to Best Avoid Rejection, Ridicule & Resistance when Prospecting People for your Network Marketing Business...
and why you've, so far, avoided telling your own sister about it!

DANNY RICH & PAUL ROBINSON

i

Published by Scaredy Cat Publishing

© 2016 Danny Rich and Paul Robinson

The authors assert their moral right to be identified as the authors of this book.

First published in Great Britain in 2016 by Scaredy Cat Publishing.

ISBN 978-0-9935718-0-0

enquiries@scaredycatpublishing.co.uk
www.scaredycatpublishing.co.uk

Contents

Acknowledgements

To Zoe, Susan, Jamie, Emily, Sam and Henry - thank you for your enduring support and understanding.

Thank you to all the amazing leaders and mentors from within our own network who have each, in no small part, inspired two working-class lads from the North of England to believe that anything is possible:

Stephan Longworth, Neil Blythe, Mark Parrish, Stephen Wharton, Helen & David Birch, Jane & Darren Turner, Kevin Hunt, Clive Leach & Diana Ross, Wes Linden, Steve Critchley, Robin Brooks, Jimmy Chapman, Chris Williams, Gary Whittaker, Mike Beeston, Louise Glaisyer, The Hon. Charles Wigoder, Andrew Lindsay MBE and Wayne Coupland.

Thank you to the following mentors further afield:

Randy Gage, Art Jonak, Eric Worre, Dr Tom Barrett, Tom 'Big Al' Schreiter, Orrin Woodward, Chris Brady, Matt Morris, the late, great Jim Rohn, Brian Carruthers, Ray Higdon, Arfeen Khan, Todd Falcone, Allan Pease, Anthony Robbins, Les Brown, Gary Vaynerchuk, Timothy Ferriss, Dr.Wayne Dyer, Bob Proctor, Rhonda Byrne (and the entire cast of *The Secret*), Brian Tracy, Jack Canfield, Jamie Smart, Jeff Olson, Michael Clouse, Richard Fenton & Andrea Waltz.

"Whatever you can do or dream you can, begin it. Boldness has genius, power and magic in it!"

- *Johann Wolfgang von Goethe*

Introduction

"He or she who shows the most business presentations, wins." - Rosetta Little.

We wrote this book out of frustration.

Not frustration at the wonderful world of Network Marketing, or frustration caused by any particular Network Marketing company. Indeed, we have spoken to many Independent Distributors from many different Network Marketing companies globally, and they have spoken of similar frustration.

Have you ever experienced the following?

A new, fired-up distributor joins your business, excited about the opportunity to change their life circumstances for the better. They "get" the business, they know what they have to do to make a success of it and they can't wait to get started.

Equally, you're excited about your new recruit. You feel that you've finally found "the one" person that is going to take the business seriously, someone you can work with, someone who is going to stick around no matter what.

Within a few short days/weeks, they're no longer taking your phone calls or replying to your messages. You're eager to catch up with them because the customers they promised to sign up never showed on your system, and the new recruits failed to materialise. What happened? Where did it go wrong?

Does any of the above describe your own experience? Yes? Well, there's good news… and there's good news!

Firstly, you're not alone. This happens throughout Network Marketing.

Secondly, the cause of this phenomenon is exactly what this book has been written to address.

If the quote by Rosetta Little at the top of this page is true (and we believe it *is*), then the first objective is actually **securing the appointment to show your business presentation**.

In Network Marketing, we do a fantastic job of equipping distributors with *skills* and *systems* that will help them to jump the 'hurdles' that they'll encounter throughout their Network Marketing career; from writing their list to overcoming objections, closing techniques, presentation skills, coaching, leadership principles…

Indeed, we seem to have a proven system for all of these areas of the business – and they work fantastically well, in the main!

Strangely, for some reason, we don't seem to have any such system for helping distributors make initial sense of their contact list.

Astonishingly, in many cases, the actual process of securing the appointment seems to be glossed-over with a *"just say these words, in this order, to as many people as you can, regardless of your relationship with them"* approach, in a rush to get new recruits into action as urgently as possible.

And this is our overriding frustration:

In the rush to get into action, not enough forethought is put into what we are going to say to prospects before we say it. In fact, in a profession of systems and procedures, this part of the process - the most important part, lacks any sort of real system beyond:

1. *Write your list*
2. *Call people from said list*

Often, new recruits are unleashed with the most basic of training and encouraged to *pitch everyone over 18 with a pulse – starting with their closest family and friends.* You know the script, something along the lines of:

"Hi, Tina. This is just a quick call. I've started this new business and I'm really excited about it. I believe there could be some benefits in it for you. How soon can I call round? I'm available Tuesday morning or Thursday afternoon..."

And this is where new distributors fall over. As great as this script is (used in the right context), *how many people speak to their closest family and friends in this manner, really?*

The response that they get is what often drives them out. They fail to clear that very first hurdle. Yet, we continue to send new recruits into the field, charged with approaching their nearest and dearest, using this script *verbatim.* There is little, if any, consideration given to *existing relationships* and how people *usually* communicate with each other, which invites **resistance**, **suspicion** and, often, **ridicule** from their prospects.

If the resistance, suspicion and ridicule they encounter doesn't drive them out of the business entirely at this stage, new distributors are often seduced into the *cold-market* where they find themselves cold calling, door-knocking, stood alongside a stand in a field approaching perfect strangers or, even worse, paying out not insignificant sums of money to advertise in newspapers and online pay-per-click campaigns... *then they quit anyway!*

Yet, MLM guru Dr Tom Barrett put it so succinctly when he said, *"We are paid for access to our lists."*

If companies wanted you to approach the cold-market, they'd miss you out completely and go there directly themselves. Your relationships with people and the trust that you've built up over the years is what they are paying you for.

Before any other skills, new distributors MUST first be taught the skills of how to approach their warm list to minimise resistance, suspicion and ridicule - which brings us to the whole purpose of this book:

How to get appointments with the people you already know.

By reading this book, you will learn a **system** that teaches you:

- How, when it comes to prospecting scripts, **one size does not fit all**
- How to **prospect everyone** on your contact list using an approach that is based upon your **existing relationship** with them
- How to overcome the **mental brick wall** that many distributors hit when deciding who to contact first
- How to go back to people who you've already '**blown out**'!
- How to **reframe your thinking** about your contact list *before* blowing them out!
- How to approach your closest family and friends and avoid coming across as '**salesy**' or weird, given that '**you only get one chance to make a first impression**'
- How to overcome the *fear* of making the initial contact with people on your list
- How to **clear the fog** of who to approach first - **and why**
- How to **identify** and **maximise** prospecting opportunities that arise within your everyday life
- How to **develop relationships** with people, over time, that will make it feel completely natural to share your business opportunity with them
- How to get prospects to **ask you** about your business

- How to successfully approach those **intimidating people** on your **chicken list**
- How to get your new team members **into action** and off to a **resistance-free** start
- How to **reduce** the chances of new team members quitting by teaching them skills that will get them off to the **best possible start**
- How to **embrace rejection** by building an effective '**No For Now'** list.
- How to **duplicate** these philosophies and skills through your team
- How to **minimise resistance, suspicion** and **ridicule** from the people who know you best
- How to **combat the fear** of approaching people with the help of **helium balloons!**

It is our sincere belief that:

The <u>key</u> to significantly improving the chances of getting our information in front of a prospect is in understanding that the language and script we use should be relative to the existing relationship we have with the prospect.

And that statement is precisely what this book is written to address. It isn't about leadership, or the customer presentation or how you should react when your *'next superstar'* suddenly quits and joins another company. They're hurdles further down the track and are the job of your company's training. The aim of this book is simply to help you make sense of your warm list, to see your relationships with people for what they are – *varying in their formality* – and, as a result, *so should your approach be.*

Using '*The 5 Levels of Formality List Profiling System'* we'll be distinguishing the differences in approach when prospecting your brother, that friend you've not seen for more than a year, the mother of your child's friend that you see at school every day, the guy who delivers your parcels and your intimidating ex-boss – and we'll be giving you the skills to get in front of those people with your business presentation.

Written as a story, based on real-life events, we follow the transformation of Sam Hirst on his rollercoaster journey - from the highs of being an excited new distributor, to the lows of personal rejection, disillusionment and frustration - and finally through to becoming an accomplished and successful Network Marketer.

Remember:

"He or she who shows the most business presentations, wins."

Danny Rich & Paul Robinson, February 2016.

1

"It's a no-brainer!"

I'd just opened my first bottle of beer and switched on the TV after a long day at work when, out of the corner of my eye, I noticed my phone illuminate. It was Barney, my best friend since I was five years of age.

"Sam, are you at home?" he instantly questioned, without even so much as a "Hello".

"Yes, why?"

"Put some coffee on, I'm on my way over. I've got something to show you. I'll be there in five minutes."

Before I could even spit out the words *"What is it?"*, he'd hung up on me and the phone went dead. My first instinct was to return his call to question him about what it was that he was in such a rush to show me, but he was my best friend and it was always good to see him. The kids, Emily and Jamie, loved him and he was always good for a laugh. In any case, he'd be here in five minutes. Knowing Barney, it was his latest hare-brained scheme that he wanted me to buy into. The least I could do was humour my best friend.

No sooner had the water boiled than Barney marched into the kitchen. He never used the doorbell, he just let himself in. That was just the nature of our relationship.

"Right, Sammy Boy, I can't stay for long, I just need to show you this," he said, in an unusually direct manner.

Barney took out his phone and handed it to me. "Press *'play'* on that video when you're ready," he instructed.

I did what I was told and watched a seven minute presentation video about science's latest health products that would help people to lose weight, look younger, lower their cholesterol, and extend their lives.

"So, those are the products," Barney said proudly. "What do you think?"

I had to admit that I was impressed with the products (if they were all they were claiming to be), and said that my wife, Zoe, would probably be interested in buying some from him.

"We'll speak about that later," said Barney, still seemingly in a hurry. "First, I need to show you how I get paid."

"Well, okay, but there's really no need. We'd expect you to make a profit!" I reassured him.

But it was as if Barney had not even heard my words as he produced a notepad and pen from his bag and began to show me the cost of becoming a 'distributor' for these products, how much profit he'd make from each sale and, most interestingly, how he could build a team of like-minded individuals and earn a profit from their sales too.

"So, do you want to give it a go?" he instantly asked, pointing at a very impressive commission total at the foot of the page.

I have to admit that I was a little taken aback by his question. Maybe I'm a little slow on the uptake but I wasn't actually expecting him to ask *me* to become a 'distributor'.

"I've got to admit that it looks very impressive Barney and, if the products are as good as they say they are, then they shouldn't be difficult to sell to people. Are you 100% serious about building a big income with this or is it just another one of your schemes that you're going to abandon after a month?" I questioned, knowing full well how Barney hopped from one money making project to another. He was famous for it, but even I had to admit that there was something different about this one.

I'd never thought about having my own business previously, but I could see potential in this opportunity and my interest had certainly been piqued. The start-up fee was less than the cost of a night out and I really couldn't see a downside.

"Yes. 100%. It's the best opportunity I've ever seen. We can do it together and build amazing futures for our families," he insisted.

After a brief silence, I did something that was completely out of character. I heard myself say, "Go on then. It's a no-brainer. Let's do it. Sign me up!"

And that was it. Within an hour, I'd paid a small registration fee, received my welcome email from the company, along with some product information to get me started, and I'd booked onto a local training that was being held in just a few days' time.

"Welcome to my team!" exclaimed Barney, holding out his hand for me to shake. "It's going to be brilliant!"

I have to admit that I was excited about my new business venture and was raring to get started. Barney had told me to keep quiet about it for now – until we'd been on training, anyway.

"You never get a second chance to make a first impression," he said profoundly, "and they'll teach you how to approach people on training, so you don't make a mess of it. For now, simply begin to write a list of everyone you know."

Barney's words, for a change, made a lot of sense, so I resisted temptation and kept it to myself (and my wife, Zoe, of course) and commenced the one activity that Barney had suggested; I began to create a list of people that I'd be approaching after my training. The names of my family and friends went onto the list, as well as people I regularly spoke to during the day. As the pages filled up with names, I couldn't believe how many people I actually knew outside of my immediate circle of contacts.

- Mike – my butcher – saw plenty of people on a daily basis
- Laura – lady at newsagents – same reason for approaching as Mike
- Postman – didn't know his name, but we spoke daily and he was very friendly
- Dave – painter and decorator and one of the dads from school – got into a lot of homes
- Julie – one of the mothers from school who was a bit of an organiser – might be beneath her though
- Henry – another one of the dads from school. Had a good job and probably wouldn't be interested
- Ian – from the gym – might not be his thing but I'd try him anyway
- Neil – one of the dad's from Jamie's football team
- Debra – my brother's accountant – probably wouldn't have time for it though
- Joan – nursery nurse – worked long hours so might not have time

Barney had instructed me to include the name of EVERY person that I knew. So I did – regardless of whether I thought they would be interested or not.

The days quickly passed and before I knew it, it was the night before my induction training. I'd arranged to meet Barney in the hotel car park at 9.00 am the following morning, so I got to bed early in preparation for the first day of my new venture. I couldn't wait!

2

"I've started a new business…"

I felt slightly anxious as Barney and I walked into the hotel foyer. I must have passed this hotel thousands of times on the way to and from work over the years and never gave it a second thought. But here I was, on my first visit, ready to learn about launching my brand-new business. I could hear the low rumble of excited voices as we approached the conference room.

"You look terrified!" laughed Barney as he held open the door.

It was okay for him, he's already done this, I thought.

Not knowing what to expect, I paused, took a deep breath and nervously followed Barney into the room…

*   *   *

What had I been so worried about? We emerged a few short hours later feeling absolutely on top of the world. What a mind-expanding and exciting day it had turned out to be. I'd met lots of local people, with many and varied backgrounds, who had decided to start their own Network Marketing business too, and, best of all, not only did I know a lot more about the company and its products, I now had a *proven script* that I could use to approach people from my *Contact List*.

"I'm glad you told me not to speak to anyone until after today's training," I said to Barney over a drink in the bar. We had decided to have a beer and a chat before we went our separate ways for the day. "I think I would have made a right mess of it if I had started contacting people before today."

Barney put his drink down and started to play with his phone, nodding his head in agreement as he did so. I drained the last of my drink and stood.

"Thanks for today pal," I said as I offered Barney my hand. "It's been awesome, and I'm going to get started as soon as I get into the car."

"No worries, mate," replied Barney as he shook my hand, putting his phone to his ear at the same time. "Glad to have you on board. Catch you later."

As I walked to my car, I realised it was now my turn. I had completed the training, understood a lot more about the company and the benefits of the products, and now, armed with a *script*, the shackles were off and I could finally tell the world about my new business. So, who better to start with than my Mum? She was the obvious first choice, so as I left the hotel car park and turned onto the dual carriageway, I gave her a call.

There was a short crackle and then the dialling sound. Mum picked up straight away. Her voice sounded slightly robotic over the car's hands-free kit.

"Hiya love, how are you?" she asked.

Here goes, I thought. I had the script on the passenger seat next to me.

"Hi Mum," I read, slightly nervously.

"It's just a quick call. I've just started a new business and I'm really excited about it. How soon can I pop over and show you what I'm doing? There'll be some real benefits in it for you."

"Oh," said Mum hesitantly. "A new business? Erm, you can come around now if you like. Is everything alright?"

"Yes, we're all perfectly fine," I said smiling. "Put some coffee on, I'll see you in a minute. I'm only around the corner."

This is easy, I thought. *One call, one appointment! 100% success so far, and it's entirely up to me how fast I can grow this thing! Bring it on!*

An hour later, I returned to my car with a bellyful of my Mum's finest lemon drizzle cake and my very first product order. Just as I'd been told earlier in the day, the presentation tools the company provided me with did the job perfectly, and whilst she didn't want to become a distributor, my Mum happily agreed to become my very first customer.

Flushed with success and optimism, I decided to make another call before I finished for the day. As I pulled my car onto the driveway, my sister Katie's voice came over the speaker system.

"Hi, sorry I can't take your call, leave me a message," she said breezily.

"Hi Katie, it's only me. It's just a quick call. I've just started a new business and I'm really excited about it. How soon can I pop around and show you what I'm doing? There'll be some real benefits in it for you. Give me a call back."

I ended the call and sat back in my seat, my car headlights illuminating the garage door of our modest 3-bedroom semi. I've never considered myself to be a particularly ambitious type, but some of the stories I had heard today, about people's lifestyles, had started me dreaming about what could be possible for my own family.

It won't be long until I'm earning enough for us to move across town to that new development of 5-bedroom executive homes, I thought to myself.

I couldn't wait to get inside and tell Zoe about my fantastic day and how I had laid the first bricks of our, *soon-to-be*, empire.

3

"You're no salesman!"

I awoke bright and early for work with a definite spring in my step. Yesterday had been a fantastic day. I'd attended a training course for my new business, I'd pitched and signed up my first customer (my Mum) and I'd left a voicemail for my sister, Katie. She'd likely get back to me at lunchtime – that's when she often texted me – and I'd planned to go around to her house to sign her up as a customer or, even better, as my first distributor, that evening.

The next person on my list was John, my elder brother. I decided to ring him on my way into the office. He was a builder. He left for work each morning at around the same time as me, so he'd probably be in his van.

"Hi John, it's Sam. It's just a quick call. I've started a new business and I'm really excited about it. I feel there could be some real benefits in it for you. When would be the best time to pop round to your house and show it to you – tonight at six or tomorrow at six thirty?"

There was a silence. It seemed to go on for an age, but it was probably no longer than 3 or 4 seconds, in truth.

"John? Can you hear me?"

"Er…yes. Yes, I can hear you…why are you speaking like that? Are you reading from a script? Why do you feel you have to ask permission to come and visit? You know you can call in anytime you like."

John's abrupt response knocked me sideways a little. I wasn't expecting that. I'd simply used the script from training and assumed it would be fine.

"Oh, okay. So I'll call in this evening if that's alright with you," I said, intentionally avoiding his awkward questions, mainly because I didn't have the faintest idea how to answer them effectively.

"Yes, I suppose so," replied my brother. "But, while we're on the phone anyway, you might as well tell me what it is you've gone and got yourself involved with."

"No, no, it'll be better if I show it to you in person," I protested, trying to cling onto any remaining control that I possessed of the conversation.

"The football's on TV tonight, now I come to think of it," he said. "Tell me what your new business is now and I can let you know if I'm interested. It'll save us both wasting our time," he insisted, stubbornly.

I was now in unknown territory. Yesterday's trainers hadn't warned us that this might happen. I was totally unprepared for this situation. I had no choice. I'd been backed into a corner by my own brother, of all people. I had to try to salvage what chance I had left and tell him all about my business, there and then. I took a deep breath…

"Well, I'm selling health products that do all sorts of things from making your hair shinier to clearing up your skin and we've got some supplements that will put years on your life as well but it's not just about selling products because you can build a team of people who can also sell these products, they're called "distributors", and when they sell products you get paid as well and when they introduce more distributors and they sell products you even get paid for that as well and there's a car plan and cruises and weekend breaks and these massive events where

thousands of distributors turn up and there's speakers and all sorts...you'd be great at it!"

"Whoa! Sam, have you finished? Take a breath!" interrupted John. "What makes you think I'd be interested in this type of thing? I eat nothing but fast food, I'm only 35, so why should I worry about prolonging my life just yet? And I'm bald! Plus, you know how seasick I get."

"I know all that," I argued, desperately. "But if you saw the presentation I was going to show you, you would see how great it is. It's about much more than the products and the cruise!"

"How good can the presentation be? It's still shampoos and pills and potions at the end of the day," he reasoned. "Look pal. You're my brother. I wish you all the best but it sounds a bit dodgy to me, so maybe you should forget about all of this and concentrate on your day job. You were telling me only a few weeks ago how there'd be a good chance of a promotion in a couple of years' time. Stick to what you're good at, *'cos you're no salesman!"* he laughed. "Anyway, I've got to hang up cos I'm nearly at work, mate. I'll catch you later, 'bye."

I was mortified. It wasn't meant to turn out like this. My own brother had turned me down without even giving me the chance to show him my presentation.

Before I could dwell too much on my disappointment, my phone began to ring. It was Phil – one of the dads from school. He was actually on my list, so maybe the powers above weren't conspiring against me after all.

"Hi Sam. Just wanted to let you know that I can collect Jamie and drop him back home after his football training with Toby tonight. I know how much of a rush it is for you after work," he said, in his usual helpful manner.

Phil wasn't a close friend, but we had our sons in common. They played football together and I often chatted to him on the side-lines.

"That'd be fantastic, Phil. Thank you. I've hopefully got a few things on this evening anyway, so that's going to be a massive help."

Then I saw my chance to instantly put to bed the absolute disaster that I'd just experienced with my brother. My script was still next to me on the passenger seat.

"Phil, whilst you're on the phone, I've started this new business and I'm really excited about it. I think there could be some real benefits in it for you. When would be the best time for me to call round to your house – tonight at 6 or tomorrow at 6.30?" I enquired – a little more nervously than before, given my recent experience.

"Sounds interesting," said Phil, to my surprise. "Tell you what. Why doesn't young Jamie come to ours for dinner tonight after football and, when you come to pick him up, you can tell me all about it?"

"Er…yes. okay. That's sounds perfect," I replied, trying not to sound too shocked. "I'll see you then."

"Yes!" I shouted out loud, after making sure Phil wasn't still on the other end of the phone. "We're back in the game!"

The disappointment of my earlier failure with my brother suddenly seemed unimportant. The conversation with Phil couldn't have gone any more perfectly. My confidence had returned quickly after that unexpected bonus. Result!

That evening, I pulled up outside Phil's home. I grabbed my folder and marched up the path to his front door. I rung the bell and Phil's wife, Michelle, opened the door.

"Evening Sam, come on in. You don't mind if I listen in as well do you?" she asked, inquisitively.

"No, not at all." I replied. "The more the merrier!"

Jamie was still sat at the dinner table, eating his dinner opposite Toby.

After the usual small-talk, I launched into my presentation. They both sat silently and intently throughout the seven minutes of my video, then watched with interest as I drew out the compensation plan on a blank page in my notebook.

"So, what do you like best?" I asked, just as I'd been taught to say at training the previous day.

"Well, I liked it all," replied Michelle, promisingly. "The products look great and I love how you can build a team and earn a residual income."

Phil nodded in agreement. This was going like clockwork. So I asked the question;

"Do you want to give it a go then?"

Michelle paused and took a deep breath.

"To be honest, Sam, I already use hair and beauty products from a lady a few doors down the road. I love the way my hair feels afterwards and my skin has never been as clear. My skin can be quite sensitive so I'd hate to risk changing products," explained Michelle, quite honestly.

"Oh...that's obviously fine. But what about the business opportunity? You liked the sound of that residual income, didn't you?" I asked, hopefully.

"I certainly did. But I've only just started a part-time job at the school and we'd really struggle for childcare if either of us took on anything more at the moment."

Again, Phil nodded in agreement with his wife.

"But we'll certainly pass your name onto people, and if anything changes we'll let you know. By the way, Jamie scored a brilliant goal at training tonight," he said, changing the subject with a finality that indicated the end of our discussion.

Only moments ago I'd thought I was certain to make my second sale or, even better, sign up my first distributor. But no. Another failure to add to my brother's earlier rejection.

I stayed and chatted for a while and left for home with Jamie. I didn't really know how I was feeling.

Did I do something wrong?

Could I have played the situation any better?

This Network Marketing game was certainly more difficult than I'd imagined.

In a bold attempt at saving the evening, I called my sister, Katie, again. Surprisingly, she'd not yet responded to last night's voicemail, so I thought I'd give her another try. After two rings, I found myself again listening to my sister's voicemail.

"Hi Sis'," I said, after the beep. "I called you yesterday about my new business. I think there'll be some benefits in it for you. Can you call me back please so that I can arrange to visit you and show you what it's all about?" I hung up, feeling more than a little despondent.

I needn't have. Within a couple of minutes, the screen on my phone lit up and my ringtone started to sound. I was delighted to see the word 'Katie' on the display and I answered enthusiastically.

"Hi Sis. Thanks for getting back to me. When's best for me to call round to tell you all about my amazing new business?"

"Hi Sam. There'll be no need. I've spoken to Mum and she's already told me all about it. I get my products from the store much cheaper than you're selling them for, so I'm not really interested – sorry love." she responded, taking the wind immediately out of my sales.

"But these are fantastic quality, Katie. You'll not believe the shine it will give to your hair and your skin will be amazing within days. I've got some free samples for you to try. Shall I drop them off tonight?" I asked, probably sounding much more desperate than I'd intended.

"No, really, Sam. I'm not interested. Even if they're the most amazing products I've ever used, I can't really afford them at the minute. I'd love to support you but you know how tight money is for me."

"Well what about the business opportunity? If you're struggling for money, wouldn't you like to earn some extra cash?" I reasoned, despairingly.

"No. All of my friends are in the same boat. They wouldn't be interested in buying the products either. There'd be no point. I'm really sorry Sam," she replied, apologetically.

We said our goodbyes and I pulled up the car outside my home. Jamie got out and went inside. I remained in the car silently for a minute or so. Zoe appeared at the door to see where I was, so I unclipped my seatbelt and trudged into the house, feeling defeated, deflated and disillusioned.

"What's wrong with you?" asked Zoe, obviously picking up on my body language. "Didn't the appointment with Phil go too well?"

"No. It went terribly," I snapped. "They weren't interested in either the products or the business opportunity."

"Well there's no need to take out your frustrations on me," she snapped back. "Why don't you see if Jack is interested?"

Jack was Zoe's elder brother. He knew a lot of successful people outside of my circle of friends. I suppose it wouldn't do any harm to try him.

"I'll get in touch with him in the morning. I'm off work anyway," I replied.

The next morning came and I had to admit that I'd perked up a bit. The sun was shining and I had a good feeling about Jack. He always seemed to be in the middle of some new business deal and lived in a much bigger house than ours, with his wife Joanne and their two boys. Surely he'd see how amazing this opportunity was. I called him at 9 am sharp.

"Hi Jack, it's just a quick call. I've started a new business and I'm really excited about it. I think there could be some real benefits in it for you. When would be the best time for me to call round and run it past you? This morning or this evening?"

"Wow! That was slick. Morning Sam. Er....I'm in this morning. Come straight over if you like. I'll get the coffee on," was his immediate, and seemingly amused, reply.

"Great, I'll see you within the hour." I said.

16

And, without a second's hesitation, I grabbed my folder and jumped into the car. That's what I liked about Jack. He didn't waste time. If there was money to be made he needed to see it as soon as he possibly could.

I entered the driveway through the already opened gates and slowly approached Jack and Joanne's house. The expensive stone chippings crunched beneath my tyres and their labrador, Murphy, began barking from within the house. Jack spotted me through the window and emerged from the house to greet me.

"Morning Sam. We've not seen each other for a while have we? We must get the families together soon. How're Zoe and the kids?"

"They're great, thanks," I replied.

"You should all come over for dinner again soon," suggested Jack. "You could stay overnight so that you and Zoe can have a drink."

"Done!" I replied.

We entered the hallway and went through into the kitchen. The smell of the coffee hit my nostrils instantly and I perched myself onto one of the three stools at the breakfast bar. The kitchen was recently installed and was looking immaculate.

"Milk, two sugars isn't it?" asked Jack, pouring coffee into the already waiting mugs.

"Yes mate, cheers," was my reply.

Jack wasn't really one for small talk so, as he walked over with the two drinks, he got straight down to business.

"So, what's this new business that you're really excited about? They've certainly got you trained with your telephone pitch, whoever it is!" he joked. I was a little embarrassed by his remark.

"Yes, it's a line they taught us on training at the weekend. To be fair, it does seem to work some of the time," I replied, defensively. "After all, I am sat here now!"

"Yes, I suppose you're right," agreed Jack, with his eyebrows raised and a hint of a smile on his face. I grabbed my phone and handed it to Jack.

"Press *'play'* on that video. It's going to tell you about the products I'm promoting."

"Okay, fair enough," he responded.

Then, after what couldn't have been more than 30 seconds, Jack suddenly pressed *'pause'* and looked at me in an *'I don't know how I'm going to break this to you'* type of way.

"I've heard of this company before. My friend, Larry, tried it once. There's no money in it, I'm afraid. It's a pyramid scam and only the people at the top make any money. You're in way too late. I wouldn't be surprised if it was illegal if I'm honest. You and Zoe are better off out of it – I'd hate to see you and my sister get ripped off," was his unflinchingly direct opinion.

"Well I've been on training and the trainers and some of the other distributors say there's plenty of money to be made – and it's not illegal – the company has been in existence for more than 20 years!" I argued back.

"Like I said. You've probably missed the boat then, Sam. Sorry buddy, this one's not for me I'm afraid."

I felt numb. *Had I joined a pyramid scam?*

I wasn't sure what one was, if I was honest, but I remembered the term from my childhood when one of my father's friends got involved in something. It didn't end well if I remembered correctly.

We finished our coffees and I made my excuses and left. I sat in the car and just stared out of the window. This feeling was now starting to become familiar to me – and I'd only been in the business for a matter of days.

I called Barney. Surely he'd be having more luck and would be able to help me.

"Hi mate. How's it going?" I asked, as he answered.

"Great, pal. How've you been getting on since the training on Sunday?"

"Not too well," I replied "I signed up my Mum as a customer straight away, but I've tried four people from my list since then and had no joy whatsoever. I'm starting to question whether I'm cut out for this type of thing. What am I doing wrong?"

"I'm not sure, Sam," was his answer. "Are you using the script from the training?"

"Yes, word for word," I assured him.

"Then I haven't got a clue. And to be honest, I was going to call you today. I'm going abroad to work for a couple of months, so I'm going to have to put the business down for a while. But I heard there is a more advanced training in a couple of weeks' time at the same venue as last weekend. Maybe you should book yourself onto that and ask some of the more experienced distributors for some advice."

19

And there he went. My sponsor, and the only person I knew in my up-line, was gone and absolutely no use to me and my new business whatsoever. Typical Barney. I started the car, drove home and booked myself onto the course that Barney had recommended.

Maybe I'll take a break from the business for a while and get back on track after the advanced training. Why continue to do it incorrectly and burn even more bridges? I thought to myself. I put my folder in an office drawer and felt an instant weight lifted from my shoulders.

I'm not quitting, I reassured myself *I'm just putting it down for a while until I've been trained a little better.*

I threw myself into my day job over the next couple of weeks. I had resolved that I was definitely going to make a success of my new business once I had done some more training, but it was also nice not to have to do anything with it whilst I waited for the training day to come around.

The truth was, I was prepared for some of the *'rejection'* I had been told to expect at my first training, but I really didn't like the way it made me feel, especially from those closest to me.

4

Camaraderie, Excitement, Optimism... Impatience

The training day came.

There was an even greater buzz around this event. It was being held in the same hotel as the first training but in one of the much-larger conference rooms. The seats were set up in wide rows of about 30, and there was easily a couple of hundred people there already. High energy music blared out of the speakers on the stage as I signed the registration sheet at the door.

I didn't recognise anyone in the room, so I took a seat about two-thirds of the way back and waited, pretending to read the notes in my folder and occasionally checking my phone. People were shaking hands and hugging each other as they arrived, and there was a real sense of camaraderie between people. I liked it. You rarely saw this kind of behaviour in the 'real world'.

"Can everyone take their seats please?" shouted a very smartly-dressed lady from the stage. "We're about to get started."

"I'm Mark," smiled the man sitting down in the seat next to me.

"I'm Sam," I replied, shaking his hand and smiling back.

"This is going to be a great day," he said.

"I certainly hope so," I replied.

And what a great day it was. Speaker after speaker took to the stage and shared their very best hints and top tips about how to build the business, and some of the stories I heard about their challenges and experiences along their journey were truly inspiring.

Mark introduced me to some of his team at lunch too, and it turned out we had a few friends in common. I was really enjoying myself, meeting new people and learning new things. All the while I could feel a strange mix of excitement, optimism, and impatience building inside of me.

"A few of us are going to try that 'Street Survey' idea that Jane talked about next Saturday," said Mark. "You're welcome to join us," he offered as we walked to the car park.

"That would be great," I replied, as we exchanged phone numbers. Of the countless ideas and tips I'd heard today, the 'Street Survey' was one that had really caught my imagination.

"I'll call you during the week to arrange it. Great to meet you!" said Mark, shaking my hand.

I left the hotel car park with a renewed sense of optimism and enthusiasm, and I couldn't wait to try my luck with the 'Street Survey' in a week's time.

I decided that, although I had learned a lot of new ideas today, I'd draw a line under everything I'd done so far and restart my business again properly next week. I was discovering that rejection from my family and friends was hard to take, and I certainly didn't want to contact any more people I knew personally and continue to make a mess of it. There were millions of the general public to talk to who surely couldn't make me feel as bad as the way my friends and family had done so far, could they?

5

Cold Market Blues

We gathered outside the bank on the high street at 8.30 am, as agreed. Four of us, wrapped up warm in raincoats and fleeces to protect us from the wind and rain, armed with a clipboard, pen, and a survey form each. The idea was to stop passers-by and ask them if they would be interested in earning an additional income without it affecting their current job.

Easy, I thought to myself, although some of my initial optimism and enthusiasm from last week's training had waned over the past week. I was feeling a little more anxious. *Everyone wants to earn more money. It won't be long before I've got a form full of names and I can get out of this cold weather and back home.*

It was much harder, much colder, much wetter, and took much longer than I expected. Getting people to stop and talk was the first challenge, as most would deliberately avoid walking in my direction or even making eye contact with me. I'm a pretty laid-back, easy-going person and don't consider myself to be forceful in any way, but I rapidly realised that stopping and interrupting strangers in the street did not sit well with my nature. I was completely out of my comfort zone.

Of those that did stop, the vast majority weren't interested in answering any questions, and many of those that did surprised me by replying that they wouldn't be interested in an additional income. I couldn't believe it. I thought everyone wanted more money!

I'd had enough by early afternoon. Cold and wet, I looked at my clipboard - I had collected just seven names of people who'd said they would be interested and would be happy to receive more information.

As I said my goodbyes to the rest of the guys (who'd had similar results), Mark said, "We've got a stand booked at a business exhibition in two weeks. Do you fancy joining us?"

This was another way of recruiting people that had been spoken about at the training last week. The man who had spoken about it was immaculately dressed and clearly very successful, and I must admit, it was another idea that had appealed to me. Unlike standing here in the street, feeling uncomfortable about interrupting people, at least the people attending would be there for business reasons.

"Yes, I'll give it a go," I replied.

I spent the next couple of days trying to contact the people I had spoken to during the street survey. Frustratingly, three of them had given me incorrect contact details (which I suspected was deliberate), two wouldn't reply to either my phone calls or emails, and one of those that did said he had changed his mind! I couldn't believe it.

My enthusiasm was on the floor as I dialled the number of Victoria, the final prospect from my list of seven. She had agreed that I could send her some further information by email. I'd done that as soon as I returned home from the street survey.

I was startled when she said she'd reviewed the information and she wanted to meet up to learn more about the business opportunity! *The fortune is in the follow-up,* I thought to myself. That was a phrase that I had heard at the advanced training and I now began to understand exactly what it meant. I found myself getting excited. My speech began to quicken as I arranged to meet her for a coffee and a chat in the foyer of the local hotel.

I suppose the meeting went well. Victoria really liked the idea of getting started with us, but she didn't have enough money for the small registration fee. We agreed that we would speak again in six months when she felt she would have the money, and she also put in an order for some products with me. She ordered one of the least expensive items, which I suspected was more out of guilt for wasting my time, or more likely, out of pity for me rather than because of any real need.

That evening I laid in bed staring at the ceiling. On reflection, as excited as I had been at times, my new business wasn't going well so far. It was certainly a lot tougher than I'd anticipated, and although I knew I had to get comfortable with rejection, I didn't like it at all. It seemed like most people weren't interested in either the products or, more surprisingly to me, earning an additional income.

So far, I had spent 2 days on training courses, half a day in the wind and rain on the High Street, and probably another day, in total, face to face with people on appointments. All I had to show for it was a LOT of rejection and two small product orders. I had earned pennies so far for what seemed like a lot of effort. I also had to hope that my Mum and Victoria liked the products enough to reorder again at the end of the month. I wasn't feeling optimistic.

But, I'm a loyal person and I also like to give things my best shot. I decided that despite the nagging doubts at the back of my mind about whether I could be successful, I would write the disappointment of the street survey off to experience and restart once again this coming Saturday at the business exhibition.

I started to feel good about the fact that the attendees would be there to look at business opportunities, so my chances of success would be much higher. I was reminded of another phrase that I had heard from one of the top earners at the advanced training, *"Fish in the right pond,"* and I certainly felt there would be more of the *'fish'* I was looking for at the exhibition.

25

6

Saturday came around quickly.

The exhibition was being held at the local football stadium in one of their large auditoriums. Mark had arrived early to set up our exhibition stand and, as I approached, I was really impressed with how it all looked. There was a lot of hustle and bustle around the room as stands were being erected and displays put together.

Our exhibition stand looked fantastic. The company colours and branding stood out proudly amongst all the other exhibitors and the product display looked equally impressive. We had each contributed £50 to the cost of exhibiting, so I was pleased with how it looked, given that I had to invest some money. Zoe and I had actually clashed about me contributing to the costs, because in her words, "it would be costing me more than I had earned."

Mark advised that the idea for today would be to chat to people that approached our stand about our products and the business opportunity, encouraging them to leave their business card in a large empty fishbowl we had placed on the table. We also had promotional pens, stress balls, and badges to give away. The main doors were open and people began to stream into the room.

I loved it! It felt like I spoke with hundreds of people and I had a great time doing it too. This was more my style! I enjoyed speaking with the attendees and not once felt like I was being a pest. In fact, *they* were approaching *me,* wanting to know more about our company.

The atmosphere between the five of us working the stand was brilliant too, and as well as making lots of new contacts, we had a great laugh together. At the end of the day, we divided the business cards equally between us and promised we would let each other know our results after following them up. I arrived home that evening with a smile on my face, a takeaway for Zoe and I, and in a much better mood than last week following the street survey.

I left it until Monday evening after work to start making follow-up calls. Although more people answered my call this time and the reception was much warmer than it had been from the contacts I had made last week, the outcome was largely the same.

Most people had read the promotional material we'd handed out or had visited our website, but had decided *'it wasn't for them'*. Some of them said they were interested but, much like Victoria, they were not in a position to get started immediately.

Mike, however, was ready. As I dialled his number, I flipped his business card over in my hand and remembered that he was someone I had spoken with personally on Saturday and we'd got on really well. He was quite an extrovert, larger than life character, who worked in sales and we had talked about lots of other things, such as football, as well as discussing the business opportunity.

It felt really good when Mike told me that he'd reviewed the information, really liked what he saw, and wanted to join. *"Yes!"* I thought, *"My first team member!"*

I emailed Mike with details of my website where he could register as a distributor and arranged to meet him for a coffee after work the following day to help him get started. Within minutes, my phone buzzed with an email from HQ informing me that a new team member had registered at my website.

I felt like I was walking on the moon as I poured a glass of wine for myself and Zoe later that evening. She giggled as we toasted my success, remarking how I was easily pleased, and she indulged me as I began to talk about all the things we would buy, the experiences we would have, and the places we would go once the team and my income had grown. My first team member was a successful salesman. How could he fail? He was going to be a superstar!

I went to bed later that night a happy man. I was on the road to success at last.

7

"This isn't sales, as such..."

The following evening, Mike was already waiting for me in the coffee shop. We smiled and shook hands as we sat down. Small talk about each of our day's events ensued.

"I love exhibitions," said Mike. "I've done lots over the years and really enjoy meeting new people. When is the next one arranged for - next weekend? I'd love to be involved with that," he continued.

"I'm not sure," I said. "As far as I'm aware, there aren't any more booked. Anyway, exhibitions are really just an additional way of building our business. The main way is through family, friends, and people we know already. You will learn a proven script for approaching these people properly at your first training."

"Oh," said Mike. "I'm a bit confused," he continued. "You mentioned you've only been involved a few short weeks yourself, but you're doing exhibitions to get leads. Have you run out of family and friends already?"

"No," I replied. "I've spoken to a few, but, to be honest, they weren't very receptive, so I thought I would try some other ways and maybe go back to them in the future."

"Then we may have a problem," said Mike. "I've not been living here long and most of my family and friends live 200 miles away. I don't think they would see me anyway. I've pitched them all many times over the years with numerous schemes and I think they just see me as a salesman now."

31

"This isn't sales, as such," I replied. "It's more like sharing the information and benefits of the products and then helping people reach a decision."

"I'm still not sure they would listen to me," said Mike. "But I can do exhibitions if I want though, right?"

"Yes, you can," I replied, "Although there are obviously costs involved in doing so. Saturday's event was almost £300, for instance."

"Oh, doesn't the company pay for that?" asked Mike.

"No," I replied. "It would be up to you, although you could do what we did and share the costs."

"Hmmm. I think I've misunderstood things here," said Mike. "I don't think this is for me. There's no way my friends and family will take me seriously, given my track record, and I simply can't afford to be forking out for exhibitions every week. What do I need to do to get my registration fee back?" he asked.

My heart hit the floor. My first distributor hadn't even got started and he was quitting already. I didn't want to lose him, so started trying to explore some ways that the business could work for him. After some fruitless pleading and cajoling, I reluctantly advised Mike to contact HQ to sort out a refund of his registration fee.

The atmosphere over dinner that night was frosty, to say the least. I decided that rather than hide anything, I would tell Zoe immediately that Mike had quit and this inevitably brought up the subject of the £50 I had 'wasted' in attending the business exhibition. I knew better than to argue with her. I let her get her opinion off her chest and said no more about it. She would calm down by the morning.

I stared at the bedroom ceiling again through the darkness. I was no further on. In fact, I was no further on and £50 worse off!

What was I doing wrong?

8

Hidden In Plain Sight

I don't know what woke me, but I looked at the clock and it showed 2:08 am. It wasn't like me to stir during the night. I was a renowned heavy sleeper.

As I turned over and closed my eyes, thoughts of yesterday's events flashed through my mind. The familiar sinking feeling in my stomach returned as I remembered how my new 'superstar', Mike, had quit − even before he'd got started.

There was a little voice in my head telling me to do likewise. *Was it really worth all of this frustration, this emotional rollercoaster that I'd not been ready for?* Maybe I just wasn't cut out for Network Marketing. I could notify the company first thing and tell them that I was quitting too.

But it was that word 'quitting' that I didn't like. My Dad had always said to me, "Son, winners never quit and quitters never win."

If only he had given me a pound coin for every time he'd said that to me in the past − I'd not be in this situation now!

And what about all of those normal, average people who *were* making a success at this? I'd seen them speaking and publicly recognised at the trainings I'd attended. And, on more than one occasion, I'd heard stories of perseverance, of how people had thought of quitting but stuck to task and eventually became winners.

No, I resolved. *I'm not quitting. Not yet, anyway.*

I was now wide awake and my restlessness was disturbing Zoe. I decided to get out of bed. I crept into my office, pulled open the top drawer and took out my notes from the trainings. I tip-toed downstairs, made myself a cup of coffee and sat on the sofa. Opening the notebook, I felt sure that there must be *some secret* somewhere – a *'golden nugget'* that I was missing.

Reading through my hastily taken notes was quite a challenge. In my eagerness, I'd clearly been in a rush to jot down as much information as I possibly could and my handwriting was barely legible – even to me. But I managed to make sense of most of it and memories of the training days came flooding back – along with the emotions of excitement and optimism that I'd so much enjoyed.

Then something struck me. I counted 1, 2, 3, 4 times. Four times, at the advanced training, it had been emphasised by various speakers that the *secret* to this business was *'your list'*.

I recall feeling a little underwhelmed when a guy who'd been introduced as *'one of the top 1% of earners in the business'* took to the stage, declaring that he was going to reveal the secret of success in this business, only to advise us all to carry a hardback book at all times, so that we could make calls from our list whenever we had a spare few minutes, within the *'nooks and crannies'* of our day.

Re-reading my notes, I noticed that I'd written down phrases such as, *'your list is your fortune'*, and *'if you haven't got a list, you haven't got a business'*.

Successful distributors had told of how they'd built their businesses in the *nooks and crannies* of *their* day; whilst the kettle was boiling, during their lunch-break and on the train home.

Either they were keeping the real *secret of success* to themselves, or what they were saying was actually true. Maybe I was complicating the issue.

That was it. My mind was made up.

Tomorrow morning (or in a few hours, in truth), was going to be a new dawn in more ways than one. I was going to do what I'd been told by the people who were where I wanted to be. I was going back to my list and Dave, a painter and decorator, and one of the dads from school, was going to be my first prospect. He was there every morning, without fail, so I was going to approach him about my business. He was constantly meeting new people through his work, so he would make a great distributor. There. Dave it is then.

I looked at the clock. It was 4:30 am. I thought it would be a good idea to sneak back to bed and grab a couple of hours sleep before the alarm sounded.

9

"Every adversity...carries with it the seed of an equal or greater benefit." - Napoleon Hill

---

I awoke to the sensation of Zoe's elbow nudging my ribs.

"Come on, sleepy-head. Time to get up."

The alarm was still buzzing. It had failed to wake me. The couple of hours of sleep I'd missed during the night had taken its toll, but I jumped out of bed with a new feeling of vigour and determination. I was going to approach Dave, the painter and decorator, this morning, and I was convinced he'd be interested.

Jamie seemed to be getting dressed and eating his breakfast even more slowly than usual, or maybe it was my impatience to get into the car and off to school. But he was ready no later than normal and off we went.

We saw the same pedestrians we always saw, passed the same cars, at the same places that we always passed them, and I pulled into a parking space in the same area where we always parked. Unclipping my seat belt, I noticed that Dave's van, with its colourful image of a paintbrush on the side, wasn't parked in its usual spot, in fact, looking around, it was nowhere to be seen.

Maybe he's running a few minutes late, I thought to myself, unconcerned.

With Jamie lagging behind, as usual, we made our way down the corridor and into the classroom. Josh, Dave's son, was already sat at his desk reading, but there was still no sign of Dave. I ruffled Jamie's hair.

"See you later, son," I said, and made my way, more slowly than usual, back to the car, on the lookout for Dave.

"Have you lost something?" asked a voice from behind me.

It was Henry, another one of the dads. His daughter, Olivia, was in Jamie's class. He was actually on my list, but I'd not approached him yet. I told myself it was because I'd not had the chance, but in reality, I knew that I'd avoided speaking to him because he intimidated me a little. Not because he was scary or unpleasant, but because he always seemed very assured, composed and had an air of affluence and success about him. Henry always wore smart clothes, sometimes a suit. His car was never more than 3 years old and I'd heard from Jamie that Olivia went on plenty of holidays. Many more than we could afford.

"You haven't seen Dave have you, Josh's Dad? I wanted to speak to him," I replied.

"No, his wife dropped Josh off this morning. I think Dave must be working away this week," he informed me, helpfully, as well as, unbeknown to him, disappointingly.

"Oh, okay. I'll catch him another time," I mustered, trying to hide my frustration.

I'd built myself up for this moment and, for the first time that I could remember, Dave hadn't been at school. Typical of my luck at the minute.

"Sounds like it was important. I've got his mobile number if you need it," Henry went on.

Despite parking my car next to his vividly illustrated van five mornings per week, I'd never taken the time to add Dave's number to my phone contacts.

"Well, yeah, sort of. But it'll wait," was my response.

"Okay, see you tomorrow then," Henry said, cheerfully.

I nodded and smiled as I trudged towards the car. Again, this business had my emotions on a rollercoaster. Five minutes earlier I'd been set to take on the world. Now, I was deflated, feeling that events were conspiring against me once again.

No! I thought to myself. *I'm not going to be like this. I'm going to take the bull by the horns, and what better way to do that than to approach Henry?*

I did an about-turn.

"Henry! Henry, have you got a minute?" I yelled across the car park.

"Yes, of course I have. What is it?" he replied, with a smile on his face.

"I wanted to speak to Dave about this part time business that I've started but he's not here today, so I'm gutted, 'cos I thought Dave would be really great at it, with him being in different houses each week, it's selling health products and stuff, it's really good, but seeing as he's not here...would you be interested in looking at it?"

What was I doing? I'd completely lost my head and failed to stick to the script that I'd been taught. Henry was going to think that I'd lost my marbles! But his response took me completely by surprise.

"That sounds interesting! We should get together for a coffee so that you can tell me more about it. Maybe I could tell you about what I do as well? We might just be able to help each other out?" he said, calmly, without appearing to be even slightly concerned at my inane ramblings.

"Er, yes. That would be fantastic!" I exclaimed, still not coming over quite as cool as I'd have liked.

"How about now?" asked Henry. "I've got a couple of hours free this morning before I go to play golf and my wife, Susan, is away having a *spa-day* with her friends. How are you fixed?"

"I don't work Thursday mornings, so yes, that would be great," I replied.

"Then follow me. Would it be okay if we met at my house? I've got a few things that I need to attend to before I head for the course."

"Yes, that would be okay. Fine. Great even!" I agreed.

"See you in five. Just park beside me on the driveway."

10

The Key: Reflecting Your Existing Relationships

It was the first time I'd ever been to a house that had electric gates. I could see them closing behind me in the rear-view mirror as I slowly ground to a halt beside Henry's silver Mercedes.

The house was a double-fronted Georgian property in one of the town's leafy suburbs, with immaculately manicured lawns and a beautiful rose garden in the centre of the circular gravel driveway. It was clearly an expensive property but tastefully done and not too ostentatious and showy. I don't know what Henry did for a living, but he was clearly successful at it, whatever it was. My mind began to race and I started to feel anxious.

I felt conflicted, too. On one hand, my gut feeling was telling me that someone clearly as successful as Henry probably wouldn't need an additional income, and he may even look down his nose at my business. On the other hand, I recalled learning at the advanced training recently that everyone should be shown the information we had to share and be allowed to decide for themselves. *'Never pre-judge'* was the phrase I remembered.

If I could get someone as successful as Henry into my team, I would no doubt make a fortune, given his success already, I thought. *I hope I don't mess this up.*

I paused and took a deep breath to calm my nerves before I stepped out of the car. The sweet aroma coming from the flower bed lingered in my nostrils as I followed Henry into the house.

"Grab a seat in my study whilst I go and make us some coffee," said Henry, smiling and gesturing towards a doorway to my left.

I entered the room and sat down on a leather sofa. There was a beautiful antique desk under the window and a high-backed chair behind it. I could see our cars through the glass.

This was clearly Henry's office, and I scanned the room as I waited for him to return. The walls were lined with bookcases, brimming with hundreds of books, and I could see some familiar titles, including some that had been recommended as *'must reads'* at my first training, coincidentally. There were framed photos of Henry and Susan and their family enjoying themselves on holiday, and formal portraits of them too.

There was also a trophy cabinet filled with lots of trophies and medals. Some were clearly sporting achievements, and others I couldn't identify, and the wall above was decorated with framed certificates. I didn't feel I knew Henry well enough to get out of my seat and inspect them to find out what they were all for, so I waited quietly and tried to compose myself ready for his return.

"Here we are," said Henry, walking into the room holding a tray. The steam rose from a cafetiere of fresh coffee, and there was a plate of biscuits, a bowl of sugar, a jug of milk, and two cups on the tray too. Henry poured me a cup of coffee.

"So, tell me all about it then!" exclaimed Henry invitingly, smiling and sitting back in his chair.

"Okay," I replied. "It's best if I let someone else do the talking, to be honest," I said, passing him my mobile phone. "Press *'play'* when you're ready."

"Great stuff," said Henry, taking my mobile.

He sat in silence for the next seven minutes, concentrating on what was coming from the screen. He would occasionally raise or lower his eyebrows and nod his head, which was the only reaction he gave during the short presentation.

"Ah, that's the company you're with," said Henry, as he returned my phone. "I felt sure you had started a Network Marketing business, and I was curious to find out which company you had joined."

"Oh, so you know about Network Marketing then?" I asked, surprised and taken aback by Henry's response.

"Absolutely. I love Network Marketing," Henry returned.

"I won't be joining your team," he continued, "but I'll happily buy some products from you, and refer you on to anyone I know who you may be able to help. I've come across your company before; it's a great company and you've made a great choice to get involved. If I wasn't already involved with a Network Marketing company, I would take a serious look at yours."

My head was spinning. *What had just happened?*

"You're in Network Marketing too?" I stammered.

"Yes, of course," replied Henry, smiling. "You seem surprised. It's a no-brainer!"

"I...I...it just never occurred to me," I said. "I thought you would be a solicitor or a barrister or some other kind of professional with all the certificates you have on the wall."

Henry laughed. "Not a chance. I've done all that professional, corporate stuff and had enough of it. No, I've been full-time in my Network Marketing business for the last five years, and the awards you see are

43

just recognition for some of the achievements along the way. Here, let me show you what we do," he said, turning his computer screen to face me.

I sat and watched a short promotional film about Henry's Network Marketing business. I was impressed. It promoted completely different products to my own company and it didn't clash with what I was doing. I had a thought.

"Can I join your company?" I asked Henry.

His brow furrowed. "Why would you want to do that?" he asked.

"Well, if truth be told, I'm not doing too great with my company at the moment, and yours looks easier, so I could run them both alongside each other and build them both together."

"If you chase two rabbits, you end up with no dinner," replied Henry.

"I'm sorry?" I asked, confused. "What do you mean?"

"I mean that you can't build two businesses at the same time. How would you know where to focus your efforts? How would you know which business to prospect? The people you are approaching, what will they think? What would it do for your reputation?" replied Henry.

I thought for a few seconds. Henry's words made sense. It *would* be confusing, and I could also imagine people would be reluctant to speak with me because it would seem like I was always selling them something. I didn't want to become a pest.

"Okay, I'll scrap what I'm doing, join your company and concentrate fully on that then," I said.

Henry smiled again. "No. I won't allow it. You're with a great company already. You just need to really commit yourself to it and focus," he replied.

Henry continued, "You said you're not doing too great just now. What challenges are you having, specifically?" he asked.

"Where do I start?" I said. "The main obstacle seems to be the people closest to me. My Mum bought some products but I suspect that was more out of pity than anything else. My brother and sister flatly refuse to even look, and my brother-in-law thinks it's a scam. Others say they don't have the time to devote to joining my business, and my one and only team member quit within 24 hours!"

"Okay, first things first," said Henry. "Some people are going to think it's a scam, and some people are going to tell you that they don't have time. Get comfortable with that because it's not going to change. The people who have heard these responses the most earn the most money."

Henry continued. "Tell me more about your brother and sister. You say they flatly refuse to even look at what you're doing, is that correct?"

"Yes. Point blank refusal. I expected more support from them," I replied.

"Tell me what you're saying to them," asked Henry.

"Well, it's a script I was taught at my first training and it goes something like;

"I've just started a new business and I'm really excited about it. How soon can I pop around and show you what I'm doing? There will be some real benefits in it for you."

"Good script," said Henry, raising his eyebrows and nodding his head. "Out of interest, is that what you were also going to say to Dave this morning?"

"Yes, pretty much word-for-word, just as I have been taught," I said.

"It's great that you're doing what you've been taught on your training," said Henry, "but you've also got to appreciate the nature of your relationship with Dave. Given that you didn't even have his phone number this morning, I imagine that Dave is a Level Three contact of yours, and that script, as good as it is, is a Level Two script," he continued. "By the same token, your brother and sister are Level One contacts and require a different approach entirely."

I was confused again. "What do you mean *Level One* and *Level Three*? Nobody has told me anything about any *Levels*," I questioned.

Henry smiled. "Let me demonstrate by asking you a question. Can you remember how you were recruited?" he asked.

"Yes, of course. My best friend Barney called me and said something like, *'put the kettle on, I'm on my way over, I've got something to show you'*. Why?"

"Classic Level One script!" laughed Henry. "Perfect!"

"Level One script?" I questioned.

"Yes. A script perfectly suited to your relationship with your best friend. You're on his first level. I take it from your expression that you've not been taught the **The 5 Levels Of Formality** principles when profiling the individual people on your List?" he replied, with a chuckle in his voice.

"Never heard of it," I said, slightly bemused.

"I can understand your frustration then," said Henry. "Here's something you have to understand:

The key to significantly improving the chances of getting our information in front of a prospect is in understanding that the language and script we use should reflect the existing relationship we have with the prospect."

I paused to absorb what Henry had just said.

"You have a close relationship with your best friend," continued Henry, "so, whether he realised or not, the best way to get you to take a look at his new business without arousing any suspicion or resistance, is to use a script that is very informal and congruent with how he would usually speak with you. And that's just what he did. Can you see how he did that?"

"I don't think there was any forethought about what Barney said," I laughed. "That's just the way we speak to each other."

"Exactly!" exclaimed Henry. "That's the key! You see, the script you're using is a great script, *but only for a certain group of people on your contact list, based on your existing relationship with them*. As I said, it's actually a perfect script for those on Level Two. If we don't communicate with people in the correct way, we invite suspicion and resistance and we seriously damage our chances of getting to see them."

What Henry was telling me was beginning to make sense.

"You're right," I said. "I used the script with my brother John and after questioning the way I was speaking, he flatly refused to see me. And my sister never returned my call after I had used that script in a voicemail message that I had left her."

"The script was a mis-match for your relationship with your brother and sister. It probably made them resistant to you because you don't normally speak with them using that kind of language or that level of formality," nodded Henry.

"Answer me truthfully – are you starting to procrastinate and beginning to feel a little reluctant about continuing to contacting people on your warm list?" he questioned.

"If I'm being honest, yes," I admitted.

My mind felt like it was beginning to clear and a weight lifted from my shoulders as I began to understand what Henry was telling me. He studied me closely before he spoke.

"I like you Sam. You seem like a good man and you're clearly a good father too, from what Olivia tells me about Jamie. I won't join your business, and I won't let you join mine, for the reasons I've already stated. What I will do though, is help you."

"Help me in what way?" I asked.

"I have some free time at the moment. How about I mentor you and teach you all about *The 5 Levels of Formality*?" replied Henry.

"You would do that?" I asked. "But there's nothing in it for you."

Henry smiled again. "I get a lot of satisfaction from seeing others succeed Sam, especially fellow Network Marketers. It would be my pleasure."

"Absolutely then!" I exclaimed.

I couldn't believe that someone I barely knew, who did not stand to benefit from it, would choose to help me like this. I was reminded of the camaraderie and mutual respect I observed at the advanced training a couple of weeks ago. This simply wasn't the kind of thing that happened in my 9 to 5 day job.

Henry laughed. "Great stuff. How about I talk you through the ideas behind the Levels and then you can go away and put what you've learned into practice?" he asked.

"Sounds great!" I said. "I've got the day off today, so that's perfect."

"Well, let's refill our cups and then we can begin," said Henry.

11

Level 1 - 'The Coffee Script'

I sat back on the sofa and raised my coffee cup to my lips as Henry spoke.

"Level One is really simple," he said, drawing a circle in the centre of a piece of paper. "This is you in the centre," he continued, writing the letters Y-O-U inside. He then drew another circle around the first one.

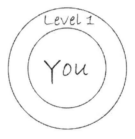

"And this ring, this *Level*, contains the people closest to you."

Henry then proceeded to write down the types of people who would typically fall within this circle:

- Parents
- Siblings
- Close cousins
- Aunts and Uncles
- Closest friends that you speak to and socialise with regularly
- Closest work colleagues
- Next door neighbour

"You know them really well and you can use the most informal scripts and language with them. They're usually family members, close friends, and people you have known for years," he explained.

"Like Barney," I replied.

"Like Barney," repeated Henry. "A typical script for someone on Level One would be something just like he used with you:

"Are you at home? Great, get the coffee on, I'm on my way over. I've got something to show you."

Anything other than this kind of language would be unusual and cause these Level One contacts to be suspicious and resistant to you because *it's not how you typically communicate with each other*."

"I understand that now," I said. "That's exactly what happened with my brother and sister. I really messed that up."

"Don't worry," said Henry. "All's not lost. I'll share with you how you can rescue that situation shortly. I take it you have actually created a Contact List?" he asked.

"Yes, of course," I replied. "Doesn't everyone?"

"Sadly not," said Henry. "And it's a huge mistake made by many. How can you profile a list into the *5 Levels of Formality* if the list doesn't exist?"

"Good point," I said. "Mine is in the car. Shall I get it?"

"Yes, I think you should," said Henry. "You can start profiling it right away."

I returned from the car with my list, and settled back on the sofa.

"Another fundamental to remember about the people on Level One is that, as well as speaking with them in the way you usually would, you should also meet them where you usually would too. Do everything you can not to arouse any resistance or suspicion from them," said Henry.

"That makes sense," I said.

"The goal is simply to share what we have with people and help them make a decision about whether it's for them or not," continued Henry. "By the way, you do realise that not everyone will join your business, don't you?" he reinforced.

I laughed. "Oh yes, I'm learning that very quickly."

"Good," he said. "Get used to it. Now, go quickly down your list and put a number '1' next to everyone you believe falls into your Level One circle. Don't worry if you've already approached them, just do it."

I scanned down my list and did as Henry instructed.

"Done," I said, counting the number of '1's I had written. "Fourteen people are on *Level One*, including those I've already messed up with."

"Great. I think we're about done for today now, so let's start to draw this meeting to a close and agree some activity ready for next time." said Henry.

"But aren't you going to teach me about Level Two and beyond?" I asked. I was eager to learn as much as I could from my new friend.

"All in good time," chuckled Henry. "Besides, you have plenty to be getting on with now and I don't want to overload you with too much information too soon. Let's master *Level One* first."

"Here's your first task: Over the next few days, I want you to make contact with ten Level One people from your List. Avoid the ones you have contacted already for now. Before you make contact though, I want you to think about how you normally speak with and act around each person, developing a script based upon that."

"Who's the first person on your List?"

"Ian, my gym buddy. We spot for each other at the gym three times a week. We meet every Monday, Thursday, and Saturday," I replied.

"Okay," said Henry. "How about a call along the lines of *'Hi Ian, after the gym on Saturday, don't rush off. I need to grab a coffee with you, I've got something to show you'.* Does that sound natural and how you would normally speak with Ian?"

"Pretty much so," I replied. "There's a café at the gym where we've occasionally had a drink afterwards. But what if he asks me what it's all about?"

"This is where you must keep your posture," said Henry. "You must show your business on your terms and not his. Tell him '*it's a visual thing and you can't do it justice over the phone*'. Don't, under any circumstances, feel pressured into expanding on what you have already said."

"That makes sense," I said. "I think I can do that."

"Who else is on your List?" asked Henry.

"Diane, our best friend from our schooldays," I replied.

"So you've known each other for years?"

"Yes, we met when we were ten years old, and we still see each other all the time," I said.

"So, would the *'put the coffee on'* script that Barney used with you be suitable in this scenario?" asked Henry.

"Definitely," I replied. "That's *exactly* how we speak with each other. And looking down this List, it would also be perfect for Paul and Rachel, Andy and Clare, Becky, Alan, and Shahzeena and Haroon."

"Fantastic," said Henry. "Is that everyone from your *Level One*?"

"Not quite. There's Vinnie I go fishing with, Dean I meet at the football, and Dan I drink with at the pub on a Friday night," I replied.

"Okay," said Henry. "Now you are beginning to understand the principles behind the first *level of formality*, let's see if you can develop appropriate scripts for Vinnie, Dean and Dan too. Remember, it's likely you would be really informal, even assumptive with these people, so develop a script that is consistent with this behaviour. Is that clear?"

"It is now," I replied, suddenly feeling energised.

"Just one thing, I usually contact these guys by text message. Can I still use the scripts in this way, or must it be a call?" I questioned.

"Absolutely. As I said earlier, you need to do everything you can to avoid arousing any suspicion or resistance, so it's important that you contact people in a way that is congruent with how you normally would," replied Henry. "So, if you usually communicate with these guys through text message, then it's crucial to do the same when approaching them with a view to looking at your business."

"That makes perfect sense," I said. Something else suddenly occurred to me.

"How do I go back to my brother and sister, who I've already messed up with, and who have their own preconceived ideas about what I'm doing? If I use the *'coffee script'* on them, they'll easily see through what I'm doing and continue to resist."

"Ah, I said we would come back to this challenge," said Henry. "An alternative approach is required for those who we have already 'messed up with', or those who have even refused to see you. I call it the **'Rescue Script'**, and it's perfect for those who fall into Level One."

"Like my brother?" I said.

"Like your brother," repeated Henry. "None of these scripts are foolproof or guaranteed to work 100% of the time," he continued, "but they do increase our chances of getting in front of people."

"But if my brother has refused to see me, how can I overcome that?" I asked.

"By acknowledging that it is unlikely that the business opportunity is going to be of interest to him and taking the pressure off," replied Henry. "It goes something like:

"You know I've started something part-time. To make it work, I've got to show everyone I know to get the word out there and naturally, being my brother, you're on my list. It really doesn't matter to me whether you join or not, I just need to put a tick or a cross next to your name once I've shown you properly. How soon can I pop around for 20 minutes?"

"I can see how that might work," I said. "I guess it puts him at ease because I've already said it's okay for him to say 'no' to me."

"Exactly. He's your brother, he cares about you so you can naturally presume that he would do you the courtesy of at least hearing you out," explained Henry.

"And, what often happens, when we use the tools that professionally demonstrate what we do, is it crushes their pre-conceived ideas and opens them up to looking at it more objectively. You will pick up new customers *and* distributors doing this," said Henry.

"So, I haven't burned my bridges with all my close friends and family just yet?" I laughed.

"Not quite yet," laughed Henry in return. "How about we meet in seven days' time back here and we can review your progress?" he continued, holding out his hand for me to shake.

"Definitely," I said. "I'll look forward to it. And thank you for this, Henry. My only concern is that, knowing my brother, he will push me for more information over the phone."

"As I said earlier, it's paramount that you maintain your posture and control of the conversation and say this, word for word:

"It's a visual thing, I can't do it justice over the phone."

"Now, if I don't get a move on I'm going to miss my tee-time," said Henry, deftly manoeuvring me towards the front door.

"So, your task for the next week is to speak to at least ten *Level One* contacts, using scripts based on the skills that we've discussed this morning, and come back with your results this time next week," Henry recapped, as I headed for the car.

"I'll get onto it right away!" I promised, enthusiastically. "I can't wait to get started – thank you Henry, and I'll see you next week."

12

Being Myself... It Works!

Wow! I thought to myself, *This new way of looking at the contacts on my list has really got me thinking. Maybe one size doesn't fit all as far as scripts go. Perhaps that goes some way to explaining my mixed results so far!*

I was still sat in my car on Henry's driveway, planning my next move. The concepts that Henry had shared this morning made so much sense. It seemed so obvious. My close family had clearly been *'spooked'* by my formal approach and, if I'm honest, I'd have probably reacted in a similar fashion had the roles been reversed. I wasn't going to make the same mistake with my remaining close friends, or *'Level One contacts'*, as Henry now had me calling them.

I decided to take immediate action. My first call would be to Diane. She was a lifelong school friend of both myself and Zoe's. I took a deep breath, ran through the *'put the coffee on'* script in my head and called her from my mobile.

"Hi Sam, how's things?" she answered, after a couple of rings.

"Hi Diane. I'm absolutely fantastic! Listen, it's a quick call. Are you at home right now?"

"Yes. I'm in all day, at least until I go to pick the kids up from school this afternoon."

"Great," I replied. ***"Put the coffee on, I'm on my way over. I've got something to show you."***

And with that, I hung up and finally reversed off Henry's driveway. So far, so good!

I knocked on Diane's door and let myself in. "Hello!" I shouted. "It's only me."

"Morning, Love. The coffee will only be a couple of minutes. Do you want something to eat? I can make you some toast if you like? Have you had any breakfast?"

"No, no, I'm fine thanks," I answered. Diane had always been something of the 'Mother Hen'.

"Okay, if you're sure. You were a bit abrupt on the phone. You didn't even tell me what it was you wanted to show me," Diane went on.

"No, it's a visual thing. I wouldn't be able to do it justice over the phone," I replied, as taught, verbatim, by Henry.

"Oh, okay. That makes sense I suppose. Anyway, what is it then... now you're here?" she questioned, handing me a coffee in my usual mug.

"Here, have a look at this," I said, handing over my phone with the opportunity video already loaded up.

"Just press *'play'* and, if you've got any questions, I'll answer them afterwards," I directed, my new-found assertiveness taking me a little by surprise. After 5 minutes or so, Diane handed the phone back to me.

"Mmmm, I like the look of that. So you're selling these products now then, are you?" she asked, very matter-of-factly.

"Well, yes, I'm *promoting* them, as well as the day job, for the time being," I corrected, "and I need to show you how I get paid for doing it as well."

I began to draw out our compensation plan on a blank piece of paper. Diane listened intently throughout, only asking a handful of questions as I concentrated like never before on getting the numbers correct.

"So, do you fancy giving it a go then?" I asked, as I drew the presentation to a close. I remember from training that, once I'd asked this question, I should resist the urge to *'vomit all over'* Diane, which was an amusing, if somewhat vulgar phrase. It was used to describe a very excited distributor who'd lost their composure and thought that telling their prospect every single detail about their company, in as little time and as few breaths as possible, would be a smart idea.

"The next person to speak loses control of the conversation," I remember being told. So I kept silent, for what seemed like an unnatural length of time, but was probably no more than 2 or 3 seconds, in truth.

"Well, I like the look of those products. Is Zoe using them?" she enquired.

"Yes, and so am I," I replied immediately, although, in truth, Zoe had resisted a little at first. Once I had explained to her the importance of being *'a product of the product',* and she had started to enjoy the benefits of using them, she soon became more supportive. Again, from the training, I remember one of the top earners saying that *'you'd never see a Mercedes salesman driving a BMW'.* I totally understood the analogy, and maybe now was the time for us to throw out all of those cheap shampoos and shower gels from the bathroom cupboard, once and for all.

"I'll tell you what…I'll try the products for a month, see how I get on with them and, if I feel that I can have confidence in promoting them, I'll be a salesman, like you," she declared. "I could do with making a bit of extra cash."

"That's sounds fair enough to me," I replied. "But I'm a *distributor*, not a *salesman*," I corrected, immediately. "Shall I grab you a month's supply from the car? We have a special promotional pack."

"Yes, why not?" Diane replied.

And with that, I'd got myself another customer, with the future prospect of her becoming a distributor in a month's time.

Driving away, although I'd only bagged myself a customer and not the top prize of a new distributor (just yet), I felt immense satisfaction in how it had gone. It'd just felt like I'd dropped in on a close friend for a coffee and showed her my new business, which, when I thought about it, was exactly what I'd just done. I really loved the concept of speaking to people on your usual terms and not being *overly-formal* with them. It felt much more natural and comfortable.

That evening, I tried the same *'coffee script'* on good friends of ours, Paul & Rachel. I didn't have as much success this time. Although I again succeeded in getting the appointment, Paul actually made fun of my new business, claiming, tongue-in-cheek, that it was a *pyramid scam*. But I'd seen, first hand, the home that Network Marketing had built for Henry, so, respectfully, I wasn't going to be put off by Paul, who constantly complained at how broke he was. He was a close friend, but his opinions on finance and business weren't ones that I held in high regard.

Nonetheless, Rachel bought some products, although the idea of them becoming distributors was a non-starter. They simply couldn't put their hands on the registration fee at that moment.

Next up would be Ian, my gym buddy. We were due to spot for each other this coming Saturday, so why not use Henry's script, word-for-word, and see how it would go? I found Ian's number in my phone and pressed *'call'*.

"Hi Sam, how's things?" he immediately asked.

"Fantastic mate. Listen, I need to be brief because I'm in a hurry. After the gym on Saturday, don't rush off. I need to grab a coffee with you. I've got something to show you." I was reading from the notes I'd taken at Henry's house. To me, this sounded slightly abrupt, but I didn't want to deviate from Henry's script.

"Ok, of course. What is it?" he asked.

"It's a visual thing and I wouldn't be able to do it justice over the phone. I only need 15 minutes of your time. And by the way, we're really going to be working on those quads on Saturday. Be prepared for some pain!" I joked, naturally changing the direction of the conversation.

"Yes, I've remembered. I've been dreading it all week." he replied.

And that was that, another presentation in the diary, and it never felt anything other than a normal, everyday conversation.

Over the next few days, I practised the *coffee script* on more of my *Level One* contacts, using a mixture of ways to reach them, including text, social media, and, of course, telephone calls, based upon how I would usually communicate with them.

- Shahzeena & Haroon – bought products, but didn't have the cash to be distributors
- Adam – wasn't interested in either the products or the business opportunity, but promised that he'd pass my details onto his mum
- Clare – bought products, but didn't have time to consider the business due to childcare issues
- Andy – neither the products nor the opportunity *'were his type of thing'*

The final one on my list, marked *coffee script* was Becky. She was a close friend of Zoe's, and she immediately agreed to see me.

Sat at her breakfast bar with a coffee, Becky seemed really interested in the video. She handed the phone back to me and her response took me by complete surprise.

"Yep, those products look fantastic and I want to try them, but first, I'd rather find out how *you* get paid for selling them."

"Er...okay. Well, for a start, we don't *sell* them, we *promote* them and..." I started, somewhat defensively.

"Yeah, yeah. Selling, promoting, whatever. How much do you get paid?" she interrupted, impatiently.

"Well, let me show you," I responded, trying to keep my composure.

The next few minutes were spent explaining the compensation plan to Becky. Dauntingly, she asked a couple of questions, but I found that I answered them with ease. I was just about to ask the big question of, *'so, do you want to give it a go?'*, when she beat me to it.

"Great. Where do I sign up?" she asked, in her typically no nonsense manner.

I couldn't believe it. It had all happened so quickly – like I'd missed something out. *Surely it couldn't be this easy?*

I took my tablet from my bag, logged onto my personal distributor website and proceeded to make Becky my second distributor.

Having been disappointed only last week by Mike, I was a little cautious.

"Listen, Becks. You do know that the only way to build this business is to make a list of everyone you know, arrange to go out and see them and then show them what we do, don't you?" I pointed out, nervously.

"Yes, like you did to me? Like we're doing now?" she replied.

"Er, well, yes. Exactly like that. Like this, even," I realised.

"Well I've got loads of friends who'll either want to use these products or join the business…or both," was her confident, no nonsense response.

Having booked Becky onto the next available classroom training, I left for home, feeling elated, but slightly cautious. I'd been down this road before, with Mike, only to be left frustrated and disappointed just 24 hours later.

Something occurred to me. *The penny dropped; I had met Mike at a business exhibition and he had wanted to grow his business by duplicating what I had done. When it became apparent that this wasn't so easily duplicable, for reasons of cost and time, he changed his mind about being a distributor. I'd introduced Becky however, using a totally duplicable way taught to me by Henry, which she would also be able to copy and put into practice with ease. It occurred to me that it was crucial to recruit people in a way they could easily duplicate.*

"Stop worrying. You did everything by the book," I said out loud to myself.

So, that was the *coffee script* exhausted. Now I'd be on my own, approaching Level One prospects just the same, but I would be composing my own scripts to suit each relationship.

First was Vinnie. We went fishing together regularly. *How could I create a Level One script based on our relationship?*

We usually met at the lake, but if one of us arrived earlier than the other, we'd go and find a couple of suitable spots, 'tackle up' and start fishing regardless. Certainly, I didn't want Vinnie to be fishing when I got there because his mind would be on the water, not on my presentation.

We usually communicated through text message. So, using the skills I'd picked up recently from Henry, I devised something that I thought would suit. I tapped it into my phone and hit *'send'*.

"Hi mate, if U get 2 the lake B4 me this weekend, wait for me in the car, got something I need to show U."

"Wot is it? That new fishing reel?" was his immediate reply. I paused to consider what my response should be.

"Nothing to do with fishing. It's a visual thing. Won't be able to do it justice by text. Will only take me 10 mins", I texted.

"No worries. C U there buddy", Vinnie returned.

I suddenly felt a real sense of achievement. I'd taken what I'd learned from Henry, used the basics and adapted it to my relationship with Vinnie – and it had worked – *Hook, line and sinker*, I thought to myself, chuckling at my unintentional, fishing-related, pun. Best of all, it had been the most natural conversation imaginable.

Next up was Dean, who I went to the football with, and then Dan, who I saw at the pub each weekend. I also usually communicated with these guys via text.

I thoughtfully composed the following scripts and, like clockwork, bagged myself another couple of *Level One*, informal business presentations:

"Hi Dean, will be arriving 15 mins earlier 2 pick U up 4 the match this wknd. Need 2 pop in and show U something B4 we set off. Is that OK?"

"Hi Dan, can I meet you @ the pub @ 7 instead of 730 this Friday. Need 2 run something by U B4 the rest of the lads get there."

Over the next few days I had mixed results with Ian (my gym buddy), Vinnie (my fishing partner), Dean (who I went to the football with) and Dan (who I met at the pub). All four of them saw my presentation, but Vinnie, Dean and Dan simply weren't interested. Ian, who I had agreed to meet after our workout, was another matter entirely;

I sipped my coffee out of the paper cup as Ian watched the last few seconds of the video on my phone.

"So, you're doing this now then are you?" he asked, giving very little away.

"Yes. I've not been doing it long, but I'm taking it very seriously," was my reply.

"So, how much money can you make from it?" Ian questioned further, dunking his protein bar into his tea.

"I was coming to that," I replied, picking up my pen and notepad.

Explaining the compensation plan was now starting to become second nature to me. The facts and figures were ingrained into my memory from the numerous presentations I'd given recently, and I found that I was able to make significant eye-contact with Ian, as I stressed the most life-changing points. My recent successes had given me a confidence and assurance that seemed to relieve the pressure from the situation. What Ian was seeing now was *'me'*, completely focussed and energized with the opportunity that I was exposing him to.

"So, do you want to give it a go?" I asked, having given Ian a few seconds to digest the potential future earnings of the business.

"Would you be there to help me along the way?" he asked, seemingly impressed by my professionalism.

"Yes, of course. Why wouldn't I be? We'd be in this together, so you would never be short of someone to guide you as you built your business," I reassured him.

"Then yes, go on then. I think I want to give it a go. If the worst happens, I can only lose the registration fee, can't I? And you can really make those amounts each month?" he questioned, excitedly.

"Yes, and yes!" I responded. "You've really got very little to lose, but those earnings can only be reached through hard work, perseverance and being teachable," I reinforced.

I was suddenly finding myself sounding quite knowledgeable, confident and assured. For the first time, I felt like I was leading someone, and the thought of helping one of my best friends to become successful and financially independent appealed to me immensely.

I recruited Ian into the business, secured him a place on the same training that Becky would be attending, and left the leisure centre with a huge spring in my step, *despite the intense battering my quadriceps had taken during the workout!*

Overall, I'd had a mixed week. Out of 11 appointments, I'd only managed to recruit two people. I really hoped that Henry wouldn't be too disappointed with me when we met up next.

13

Realistic Expectations

Thursday morning had come around quickly after a busy week. As I drove over to Henry's house, I reflected upon my activity since our last meeting and wondered what his response would be to my mixed results. I felt conflicted – I'd had some success, but also a lot of rejection too.

"So, how are things?" asked Henry, as I poured milk into the steaming cup of coffee he had just handed me.

"Not too bad, I think," I replied. "It has certainly felt a lot easier speaking with people in the way you coached me," I continued, "and I haven't really felt any awkwardness, resistance or hostility from anyone, which has been great. That said, I've only managed to recruit two new team members despite having a really busy week."

"Tell me more," said Henry. "How many calls did you make over the last week?"

"Eleven," I answered.

"Great, but the important thing is how many appointments you secured?" probed Henry.

"Eleven," I replied.

"Awesome. Well done you!" he exclaimed. "Eleven calls and eleven appointments. First of all, let's celebrate the fact that you managed to skilfully get in front of eleven people. That's a perfect ratio. Remember, the goal is simply to share what we have with people and help them make a decision about whether it's for them or not. It's not our job to convince people. Whether someone actually chooses to become a customer or distributor is often largely out of our hands. So, great job!"

"Okay," I said, smiling. "I see what you mean. Although some weren't interested at all, I've also picked up some customers and some potential distributors for the future too," I continued.

"So, you need to give yourself a pat on the back, my friend. You're not going to sell to or recruit everyone. Far from it," said Henry.

I smiled inwardly at the fact that Henry had called me his friend. Despite not knowing him for long, I had a great deal of respect and admiration for him and his giving nature.

"What else did you learn?" Henry asked.

"Well, it was quite eye-opening really," I said. "Although no-one was seriously rude or derogatory about what I was doing, I was amazed at the fact that some of them just weren't interested, and also how many of them simply couldn't afford the registration fee to get started. That's especially worrying."

"Yes, we discover lots of new things about our friends and family that we may never have discovered until we start something like this," said Henry. "Like the fact that, despite how often some of them moan about their 'lot in life', when we show them an alternative way forward, they just aren't prepared to work to change things."

"So it seems," I replied. "I felt sure a couple more of them would grasp the opportunity."

"It could be that, despite what you may previously have thought about them, they're just not *entrepreneurial*," said Henry. "There's no shame

70

in that. Many people like the perceived comfort, certainty, and 'security' of being an employee," he continued.

"I guess so," I said. "What concerns me more though, is the fact that, despite definitely seeing an opportunity for themselves, some of them couldn't put their hands on a couple of hundred pounds."

"Yes, I had, and in fact *still have*, some friends like that," replied Henry.

"The truth is, and you may have already heard this phrase, *'the vast majority of people are leading lives of quiet desperation inside'*, despite what you may see on the outside," he continued. "And the beauty of what we're doing in Network Marketing, is that we really can help people move away from living life like that very quickly – *if they choose to*. The fact that you've identified this is great for your *No-For-Now List*."

"What's a *No-For-Now List*?" I asked.

14

"No...for now."

"I'd go as far as to say that your *No-For-Now List* is, by far, the most important list that you'll create during your Network Marketing career," declared Henry.

"Really?" I replied. "Even more important than my list of names that I'm constantly working on?"

"In my opinion, yes," said Henry.

"You see," he went on, "your *No-For-Now List* contains the names of people who have declared their interest in your business as being just that – *no, for now.* They're the people who you've managed to get in front of, presented your business opportunity to, but they declined the chance to join."

"Okay," I said, "but why is this list more important than my other list?"

"Because of the one thing that they all have in common," said Henry.

"Which is...?" I questioned, becoming a little impatient.

"Well, if they've all declined the offer, then they all must have seen it. Which means that you shouldn't need to show them again," Henry explained.

"Let me go back to the beginning and explain the process. It should shed a little more light on the concept for you," he offered. "So, using the skills that you've developed in our sessions covering the *5 Levels of*

Formality, you secure yourself an appointment. You attend the appointment and present your business, but the prospect declines the offer of joining for reasons of finance or timing or you might just simply get the feeling that they're slightly nervous of starting their own business."

"Okay," I said, "that's pretty much what's happened on quite a few occasions so far."

"So," Henry went on, "instead of just accepting that they'll probably never join your business, you put their name on your *No-For-Now List* with all of the other people who now know what you do and how you get paid – but decided not to join just yet. But, and this is crucial, you seek their permission to keep them updated on any changes that might arise within your business in the future."

"That seems pretty simple, but what do I do with these names, then?" I asked. "I can't really keep on calling them and asking them, can I? They'd get pretty annoyed pretty quickly!"

"Yes they would. Your *No-For-Now List* is certainly not to be used to pester people," agreed Henry. "It is only to be used when a change has taken place in the business, such as a reduced-price joining fee, amazing new products or, if your company encourages it, you may have a new team member that you can place anywhere you like in your team structure – including beneath future new distributors."

"Okay, so how does that work?" I questioned.

"Well, I said that it was crucial that you gained their permission to keep them to date, so let's say, for example, that you've signed up a new team member and, for a limited period, you are able to offer to place this new team member in the business of anyone who signs up," Henry began to explain.

"You go to your *No-For-Now List* and pick the first name. The fact that they already know what you do and how you get paid makes the process much easier. You give them a call:"

"Hi, Jim, it's Sam. Listen, it's just a quick call. Do you remember when we met for coffee a couple of months back and I showed you my part-time business? I recall how you liked the idea of getting paid for other people's work? Well, I've just signed up a new distributor. She's a hairdresser and I think she's going to be fantastic at this business. Thing is, if you sign up as a distributor in the next 24 hours, I can place her within your team. Does that change anything?"

"Do you see what's happened here, Sam?" asked Henry. "Something quite monumental has taken place."

"Well, I see that it is now a much better offer for Jim – the chance to have a new distributor in his team before he's even got started," I said, getting the feeling that I might be missing something else.

"Yes, most certainly," agreed Henry, "but there is also an almighty shift in the balance of power!"

"How do you mean?" I asked, as my earlier inclination was confirmed.

"Well, when you prospect someone, there is a certain element of pressure on you – especially when you're new. As much as you try to detach from the outcome, you're doing your best to sell your opportunity in the best way that you can so that, hopefully, they'll agree to join your business, is that right?" asked Henry.

"Yes, of course, totally," I agreed, "it can be quite nerve-wracking at first."

"Exactly," said Henry. "But when you offer them the chance of a new distributor in their team – one that you '*think is going to be fantastic*', they experience a *fear of loss*."

"What's a *fear of loss*? I queried.

"It is the fear that, if you don't make the correct decision, it could come back to bite you in future," Henry explained. "In this example, Jim can't so easily dismiss the opportunity. There's a voice in his head telling him about future scenarios of bumping into you in the street and you telling him how amazingly well the hairdresser is doing in the business and that, if he'd taken up the opportunity to join, he'd be earning a significant income by now. Basically, the ball is now in his court and *he's* feeling the pressure!" Henry laughed.

"Wow," I said, "I can see how that can be quite powerful and how it would work."

"Or," Henry continued, "maybe, your company has halved the joining fee for a limited period and you recall how someone on your *No-For-Now List* just couldn't raise the cash when you first shared the opportunity:"

"Hi Sally, I hope you're well. Listen, it's just a quick call. Do you remember when I showed you that video about my part-time business? You were quite interested but couldn't put your hands on £100 at the time? Well, I didn't want you to miss this opportunity – the company has cut the joining fee to £50 for a very limited period. Shall we get you signed up right away?"

"Can you see how, after getting their permission to keep them updated, it is totally fine to approach them again in this way?" asked Henry. "And, because you've already exposed them to the workings of the business, they're unlikely to need you to demonstrate it again. You can simply sign them up online straight away, should they decide to join."

"Yes, I can," I conceded, totally grasping the concept of the *No-For-Now List*.

"Also," Henry went on, "if you get the mind-set right, it totally changes your approach to people when prospecting."

"Can you explain?" I asked.

"Well, instead of meeting someone to persuade them to join your business, your goal is now to simply put them on your *No-For-Now List*. If that is your goal from the outset, what can go wrong?" he asked.

"Well," I said, "nothing really can go wrong, can it?"

"No, unless they join your business – then you don't get to put them on your *No-For-Now List*. And I'm sure you'd be able to cope if that happened, Sam, wouldn't you?" Henry chuckled.

I laughed along with him.

"So, basically," I summarised, "I go out with the intention of simply building my *No-For-Now List*, which means that someone declining the opportunity to join my business is actually a success?"

"Correct!" said Henry.

"And the only thing that can go wrong is that they join my business – which means I can't put them on my *No-For-Now List*?" I went on.

"Correct again!" shouted Henry.

"Yes, I think I can cope with that!" I declared, with a grin.

"Now, let's crack on with Level Two of the 5 Levels of Formality," said Henry, taking out the piece of paper that he had used last week. He drew another, larger, circle around the two existing circles.

15

Level 2 - Favour & Feedback

"Level Two," announced Henry, "contains those people that you know quite well but who are perhaps not close enough to be on Level One."

He then jotted down a list of likely inclusions for this level.

- Extended family
- Distant relatives
- Past friends who you don't see regularly
- Friends of friends
- Friends of close relations
- Business acquaintances
- Work colleagues
- Neighbours that you'd ask a favour of

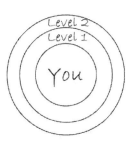

"There are people who you may have contact with infrequently, but will know you well enough to be comfortable asking you for a favour, and you would be comfortable asking a favour of them in return," he explained.

"Remember, the way this concept works is that the further away people are from you in the centre," he said, gesturing at the diagram he had drawn, "the more formal the approach and language should be with them. You would still be familiar with those who fall into your second level, but quite not as familiar with them as you are with those on Level One," he continued.

79

"I see," I said. "I can clearly understand why the script ideas for Level One are appropriate for those kind of people and don't arouse resistance and suspicion, but how can you do that with people you aren't as close to and don't see quite so often?" I asked.

"There are a couple of ways – *favour and feedback*. One is to ask for a favour," said Henry, "and another is to pay them a small, honest, and relevant compliment, and to ask for their feedback on your new venture."

My brow furrowed and I clearly looked a little confused. Henry laughed.

"Go down your list and write a number two next to everyone who you regard as a friend, but who are not so close to you that you would feel 100% comfortable using the Level One *coffee script*," said Henry. "Then I'll explain more," he said.

I spent the next two minutes reviewing the names on my list.

"There are a lot more that fall into this Level," I said.

"That's usually the case," said Henry. "If you think about it, most of us have a small circle of people that we interact with on a frequent basis. Everyone else, we know less so."

"Actually," said Henry, "before we get deeper into this; do you recall the script you were going to use with Dave that you shared with me last week?"

"Yes," I replied.

"I've just started a new business and I'm really excited about it. How soon can I pop around and show you what I'm doing? There will be some real benefits in it for you."

"That's a generic and often taught Level Two script, perfect for the people you have this kind of relationship with," said Henry, pointing to the list he had written.

"Okay..." I said, still a little confused. Henry smiled.

"Let me help you out, Sam," he said. "Cast your mind back to when you were using that script to try to get in front of your family members. How did you feel, and what kind of reaction did you get?"

"Well," I started, "I guess I felt a little odd using it because it's not language I would usually use. And as far as the reaction goes, you already know that there was a lot of resistance."

"Exactly," replied Henry. "As good as the script is, it's not suitable for the kind of relationship you have with people on your first level. It's not the usual way you speak with them or the kind of language you would use - it's too *formal*. That's why they act suspiciously and resist."

"Now, imagine this," he continued. "How would you feel and what kind of response would you expect to get using the script with these *Level Two* kind of people?" he quizzed.

I looked at the list Henry had written and imagined some different scenarios. I smiled as the realisation dawned on me.

"Much more comfortable, and I guess they would be much more receptive, I think," I replied. "I can see how a more formal approach would work in this case."

"Great, you get it!" Henry exclaimed. "Most people make the mistake of thinking that it's a *one size fits all* script. They use it for everyone, regardless of which level their prospect may fall into, and often get resistance or suspicion, just like you experienced." he said.

81

"That said," he continued, "as good as the script is, and as successful as it *can* be, I've always believed that it can be improved by investing a little time and thought into tailoring it to people specifically, which I'll explain now. How are you getting on with your list?"

"Done," I said. "There's about thirty people, I guess."

"Okay," replied Henry. "Pick one and tell me a little about them."

"Hmmm. How about Stephen, he's a friend of my brother, John? He's a self-employed plumber. The last time I saw him was about four months ago at a wedding," I offered.

"Great," said Henry. "There are a couple of things we can use here. How about:

Hi Stephen, it's Sam, John's brother. How are you?

"And then there would naturally be some small talk," said Henry, breaking out of role-play. "But once that was over, something along the lines of:

I'm calling to ask a favour. I know you've got your own business and from what John tells me you're doing well. I've just started something part-time myself, and I need to get the word out and show as many people as I can what I'm doing. Would it be okay if I pop around and see you for twenty minutes in the next day or two?

"The beauty of saying something like this is that, although it is quite normal, non-confrontational language, it is also loaded with powerful words that *put people at their ease, make them feel good, and influence them to comply with what you're asking*. All because of the way that you asked."

Henry continued, "Most people we have a relationship with are happy to do us a favour, and you make him feel good by complimenting him on the fact that he's doing well with his own business. By approaching him like this, we dramatically increase our chances of him agreeing to the favour we ask of him."

"I understand," I said, smiling as I began to grasp the subtle, hidden undercurrents to what Henry was suggesting. "He's a reasonable guy who I've always got on well with when we've seen each other, I can't imagine him refusing to see me for a few minutes."

"Great," said Henry. "And persuading him to join isn't really the goal, is it?"

"No, it's simply to share the information I have in the best way I can and then to help him reach a decision about whether this is a good fit for him or not," I replied.

"Correct!" returned Henry. "And I'm glad you mentioned sharing it in the best way you can. Although all we're doing is sharing information and collecting a decision from people, if we do it in the very best way we can, with *measured belief, passion* and *urgency*, then we significantly increase the chances of them joining us."

"I've felt myself getting more and more enthusiastic as I've been explaining it to people this week, actually," I said.

"Who else is on your list?" he asked.

I scanned down and Justin's name caught my eye.

"Justin," I said. "He's my sister's brother-in-law. Again, I don't see him often, just at family gatherings. I don't know what he does exactly, but he's a switched-on guy."

"Pretty straight forward again," said Henry. "Once you understand the principles behind the scripts, it's easy to develop appropriate approaches. Having got the niceties out of the way, I'd be inclined to go with something along the lines of:

Justin, you've always struck me as a switched-on guy. The reason for my call is to ask a small favour. I've recently started something part-time alongside my day job and I'd value your opinion on it. Would it be okay if I popped over to see you in the next couple of days to run it past you?

"Can you see how that might work?" asked Henry.

"Absolutely!" I laughed. "It's clever. It makes him feel important because I've paid him a compliment and I guess that makes him more open to doing me a favour?"

"Correct," replied Henry. "Just a measured stroke of the ego and we make him feel good, increasing our chances of success."

I nodded again.

"That's it really. Your task before we meet next is to go down your Level Two contacts and develop appropriate scripts based upon what you know about each of them, keeping the idea of *favour and feedback* in mind," said Henry.

"I can do that easily," I replied, glancing down my list.

"Now, take these new ideas, make ten more calls and we can get together again at this time next week to review your progress," he continued, standing up to indicate that today's meeting was drawing to a close.

"There's just one more thing that I need you to think about," said Henry, as we made our way to the door.

"It's fantastic that you're learning these new skills with such enthusiasm and that you're enjoying some early success, but the real secret to Network Marketing is *duplication*."

"How do you mean?" I asked.

"Well, you now have a small team of people who are about to embark on their own Network Marketing journey – treading much the same path as you did just a few short weeks ago," he began to explain.

"That's true," I replied.

"Well, what kind of start would you like them to get off to? Do you want them to encounter the same frustrations that you encountered, that nearly drove you out of the business, or do you think that you now have some skills and experience that could help them along their way?" enquired Henry.

"The second option, definitely!" I enthused, understanding entirely the point he was making. "I wish I'd heard of the *5 Levels* when I first joined the business."

"Exactly," said Henry. "So, do you think it might be a good idea to speak to your new team members as soon as possible, so that, at the very least, you can explain the first two levels, giving them the very best chance of getting their new business presentation in front of the people closest to them?" he asked.

"Absolutely! Definitely!" I exclaimed.

And with that, I thanked Henry for his time and made my way to the car with more new skills and more tasks for the week ahead – the first being to arrange a meet-up with Becky and Ian, my two new distributors, immediately after they had completed their training.

I called them both on my journey home and arranged to meet them.

16

Rekindling Friendships

I left Henry's house with an optimism and determination that I hadn't felt before. Not only did everything I had learned so far make perfect sense, I was getting the opportunity to put this valuable new knowledge into practice immediately – and it was working!

Henry had tasked me with making ten calls to the *Level Two* people on my list, of which there were about 30. I realised I was actually looking forward to doing it, and it soon occurred to me that this might be because I wasn't as close, emotionally, to these next prospects as I was to those who had fallen into my *Level One* circle of contacts.

I've always had Thursday mornings off work, in lieu of working the occasional weekend day, and in the past I had used it as an opportunity to catch up on some sleep after the kids had left for school. Spending time learning from Henry was a much more productive way of using this free time. I had about 30 minutes before I left for work for the afternoon, so I decided that I would take a quick shower to freshen-up and then make at least two calls before I left the house again.

I decided to start with my brother's friend, Stephen, the self-employed plumber. I glanced over my notes from this morning's meeting with Henry, reminded myself of the *favour and feedback* idea, and tapped in his number. He answered after one ring, catching me by surprise, slightly.

"Hi Stephen, it's Sam, John's brother. How are you?" I asked.

"I'm great thanks, Sam. What about yourself?" he replied.

"Great, great," I said, composing myself.

"I'm sorry to bother you Stephen, I know you're busy so I'll get straight to the point. I'm calling to ask a favour. I know you've got your own plumbing business and from what John tells me you're doing well. I've just started something part-time myself and I need to get the word out and show as many people as I can what I'm doing. I'd really value your opinion. Would it be okay if I pop around and see you for twenty minutes in the next day or two?"

"It would be nice to be a little busier," laughed Stephen. "Business has been a little quiet over the last couple of weeks, but it looks like things are about to pick up again," he said. "I'm not sure how much help I'll be, but of course you can come around. I'm free all day today if that suits, unless I get an emergency call-out?"

"That's brilliant," I replied. "Although, I can't do this afternoon as I've got to go into work, but I could pop by on my way home tonight. About 6.30 if that's okay?" I ventured.

"Perfect," replied Stephen, "I get back from the gym around 6 usually, so that gives me time to freshen up. There'll be a beer waiting with your name on it," he said.

"Even better," I laughed. "Great, I'll see you at 6.30. Cheers!"

"Cheers!" said Stephen.

I ended the call and glanced at the clock on the wall. I was running slightly late so decided I would make the next call from the car on the journey into work.

Once on the dual carriageway, I decided to call Justin, my sister's brother-in-law. We had exchanged numbers a few months ago whilst on a boys' weekend away. I mentally ran through the script, making sure I covered all the key points before I called him on my hands-free kit.

The dialling tone sounded three times inside the car before Justin answered.

"Heeeey!" he exclaimed. "How's it going, Sam? Have the bruises healed from the paintballing yet?" he chuckled.

I smiled as I remembered that, the last time we had been together, I had been the butt of many jokes amongst our party, having been somewhat of a *sitting duck* during a paintballing session we'd taken part in.

"Ha ha! More or less!" I countered, entering into the spirit of the conversation. "That Wooden Spoon trophy is sitting proudly on my desk at work," I continued. I don't mind being a little self-deprecating at times.

"Ha ha, brilliant," replied Justin. "This is a surprise. What can I do for you mate?" he asked.

Keeping the conversation light and friendly, I began my script:

"Justin, you've always struck me as a switched-on guy. The reason for my call is to ask a small favour. I've recently started something part-time alongside my day job and I'd value your opinion on it. Would it be okay if I popped to see you in the next couple of days to run it past you?"

"Sounds intriguing," he replied. "Of course you can, it will be good to catch up with you anyway, and it's also about time we had another night out with the rest of the lads. I'm working late tonight finalising a tender for some new business we're going after, but I'm free tomorrow after 7 if that suits?"

I pictured my diary in my mind. "Tomorrow night is perfect," I said. "I'll pop over after Emily's swimming lesson."

"Great stuff," Justin replied. "Listen," he continued, "I'd better cut this short as I've still got loads to do on this tender. I'll see you tomorrow at 7."

"See you tomorrow," I replied, ending the call.

This was going well. *Two calls, two appointments*, and best of all, everything felt natural and not at all *salesy*.

As I drove into my employer's car park, I resolved to make three more calls on my way to Stephen's house tonight, leaving the remaining five for tomorrow, before I met with Justin in the evening.

*   *   *

It was Wednesday evening. As I watched Jamie's football practice, I reflected on my progress since last Thursday's meeting with Henry.

The meetings with Stephen and Justin had gone well. I let the presentation tools do the work for me and, as I suspected, Stephen's plumbing business wasn't keeping him as busy or as profitable as he would have liked. Being the entrepreneurial type, he very quickly saw an opportunity to create another income alongside his current business (after all, as a plumber he was regularly encountering new people), and so he registered as my latest team member.

Justin was similarly impressed with the business opportunity, but couldn't commit any time to starting a part-time business at the moment, so decided not to join the team. However, he did purchase some products for his wife.

I had made all of the remaining eight calls that I had committed to do. Seven had gone really well. From these seven appointments, once again simply letting my presentation tools do the work and speaking with measured belief and enthusiasm, I had recruited two more distributors; Tony and his wife Emma, and Gareth, which made three new team members, including Stephen. A friend of my father's, Jonathan, was not interested at all, and Kevin, Mark, and Alison all appreciated the business opportunity but did not feel that it was a good time to join, given their heavy workloads. Another friend of my brother's, Craig, wasn't interested in the business opportunity but bought some products.

One call didn't go so well;

Winston was an old school friend of Katie's, my sister. We were friends on Facebook, but hadn't seen each other for a couple of years, although we had talked online occasionally in that time. From what I knew, he worked in financial services.

"Hi Winston, it's Sam," I said as he answered the call.

"Hi Sam, long time no speak!" he replied. "How are you?"

"I'm great thanks mate," I said. "I know it's been a while. Is now a good time to talk?"

"Yes, I've got a couple of minutes before I leave for my next meeting," Winston replied. "What can I do for you pal?"

"I'm calling to ask a favour actually, Winston. I've just started something part-time and I'm looking for some feedback. I know you work in financial services and understand money, so I thought you would be a good person to ask. I'd really value your opinion. Would it be okay if I pop around and see you in the next day or two and show you what I'm doing?"

91

There was a pause as Winston considered my request. "How long will it take?" he asked, hesitantly.

"An hour. Maximum," I returned.

"Hmmm..." replied Winston. There was more silence.

"I'm really sorry," he started. "I hate to have to let you down, but the truth is I simply don't have the time at the moment. There have been a lot of cut-backs at work and those of us that are left are having to take on more clients. I'm working every evening as well as during the day at the moment, and I honestly can't afford the time. I'm really sorry."

I felt a little disappointed. This was the first time the script hadn't worked.

"I can come over at the weekend if that makes it easier," I countered. "How about Sunday morning?"

"If I wasn't so busy, it wouldn't be a problem," Winston continued. "Things have been tough since the recession and we're all doing our best to try to hold things together and ride it out. Sunday is the only day I have to spend with the family. If you were to ask me again in three months' time, I'm sure I could help you," he said.

"No problem at all!" I replied chirpily, trying to hide the disappointment in my voice. "I completely understand."

"Actually, I'd better go now," said Winston. "If I don't leave I'll be late for my first evening appointment tonight. I'm sorry mate, give me a call in three months and we'll get together."

"Okay, take care," I said, ending the call.

I reflected on the conversation again as I drove to Henry's for our next meeting. To suddenly experience disappointment again when things had been going so well was unsettling.

How could I have handled the call differently? I asked myself.

I took a deep breath and tried to put it out of my mind. I pulled off the road and onto Henry's driveway.

He would tell me where I had gone wrong.

17

"Sam, sometimes the timing is just not right."

As ever, I arrived at Henry's home with a mixture of emotions.

Firstly, I was excited to discover what I'd be learning today, if our previous meetings had been anything to go by. But I was also slightly nervous. I felt I'd done okay for much of the week, having secured 9 appointments from 10 phone calls. Granted, not all of them had joined my team, but I was beginning to feel comfortable with accepting that this *rejection* was part and parcel of the business. After all, my role was simply to demonstrate the opportunity, face-to-face, and help them to make a decision on whether it was for them or not.

But there was one issue that was playing on my mind. It was Winston. He'd point-blank refused to even see me, due to his heavy workload and, no matter how hard I'd tried to secure an appointment, he stood firm.

Surely, I thought to myself, *Henry would be able to tell me where I had gone wrong and offer me an alternative script that would have worked on Winston.*

Henry greeted me cheerfully at the door. He had this knack of making me feel important, rather than someone who was imposing on his Thursday morning each week – which was how I sometimes felt.

He'd seen my car approaching the house and, as I entered into the hallway, the familiar smell of coffee and the stylish, if relaxed, surroundings somehow made me feel assured and eager to learn more about Network Marketing.

95

After the usual small-talk, Henry manoeuvred the conversation towards business – which was the real reason we were here.

"So, how has this week gone, Sam? Did you make the ten calls that I'd tasked you with?" he enquired.

"Yes, I certainly did. To be honest, after our meeting last week, I actually couldn't wait to make the calls. Armed with the *favour and feedback* technique of approaching people, I was intrigued to find out how well it would work," I enthused.

"So, are you going to tell me how it went?" Henry laughed, a little impatiently, but clearly amused at the fact that the man who, just a couple of weeks ago, was wary of picking up the phone, was now eager and enthusiastic about calling people.

"Well, since our meeting last week, I now have three new team members and two more customers," I began, trying to avoid the episode with Winston.

"Congratulations, well done!" said Henry. "But you don't seem to be as excited about that as I'd have imagined."

He was incredibly perceptive. Despite my successes this week, Winston's point blank refusal to even meet up with me was gnawing away at my mood. It was always there at the back of my mind and it made me feel that I'd still got a lot to learn about persuading people to see me.

"Well, there's one thing that's been bothering me for a few days," I began. "I phoned an old school friend of my sister's. His name's Winston and he's in financial services. We chat on social media sometimes and I felt sure he'd be a great distributor."

"Okay. Fine so far," nodded Henry.

"Well, I contacted him, complimented him on his knowledge of financial matters then asked if he'd do me a favour and take a look at my business – as I'd done with all of my other *Level Two* contacts," I went on.

"And...?" said Henry, gesturing with his hands for me to move things along, sensing that I was skirting around the issue slightly – which I was.

"Well, he said that he was too busy to even spare me an hour because of his increased workload. So I told him that I could do evenings and weekends – even Sundays, but he said that he simply didn't have time and that Sunday was his 'family day' and his only day when he didn't have to worry about focussing on work," I explained, reliving the frustrations of the conversation and getting a little worked up.

"Henry, where did I go wrong? Out of 10 phone calls I got 9 appointments, but I've gone through the conversation with Winston over and over again in my head and I'm not certain of why I failed. Maybe I could have suggested meeting him really early in the morning or even during his lunch hour, but I didn't think to suggest that at the time. Do you think I should call him back and suggest those options, or do you have another script that is certain to work? I'm sure you do..."

I could hear myself sounding desperate, but surely Henry would have secured the appointment and I was eager to hear how he would have handled it. Henry interrupted me, mid-sentence.

"Sam, Sam, just stop right there!"

He was quite forceful, but still smiling, nonetheless. "So, let me get this right. You made 10 calls, as we'd agreed. You secured nine appointments and did nine presentations. Three of those became new team members and two others bought products from you. Is that correct?" he asked.

"Yes, that's correct," I replied, sheepishly. "But Winston refused point-blank to even..."

"Enough about Winston!" Henry again interrupted, raising his voice slightly for the first time since we became friends.

"Firstly, well done – on all ten calls – even the one with Winston!" he said, encouragingly.

"You spoke to people on Level Two, used the techniques I taught you only a week ago, and your business has moved forward significantly," he went on. "Now, if we must, let's discuss the *issue* of Winston."

He stressed the word *issue* as if he didn't really think that it was an issue, but I was intrigued, if not a little desperate, to find out how he would have approached it.

"You used the *favour and feedback* technique, tailoring it to him personally, which was perfect," he began. "But he told you that he was currently under a lot of pressure at work and that now was not a great time for him to look at your business, is that correct?" he asked.

"This is where it went wrong!" I interjected. "What script would you have used to convince him to see me this week?"

"Well, this is what I would have said at that point," Henry said, looking me straight in the eyes and pausing for a couple of seconds.

"Winston, that's absolutely fine. With your workload, the timing is clearly not right for you to see me at the moment. Would it be okay if I called you back in say, 3 months' time, to see if you can spare me an hour or so? Your feedback is really important to me."

I looked at Henry. He just smiled and shrugged.

"Sam, sometimes the timing is just not right. Winston had explained to you that he couldn't fit you into his busy schedule at the moment, so the best thing is always to back off, show some respect and understanding for their situation, maybe compliment them again and arrange to call back at an agreed time in the future. You can't win them all, my friend!" he exclaimed, smiling at the situation.

As ever, he was speaking perfect sense and I could now see that, in my eagerness to arrange appointments, I'd failed to recognise that other people have busy lives and schedules too, and that 'now' wasn't always the perfect time.

"If I was to critique you on anything," Henry continued, "it would be that, in your desperation, you became a little 'pushy' and, instead of accepting the situation for what it was, you allowed yourself to persist and strive for an appointment at all costs. We must retain our posture and composure at all times," he explained.

I understood and agreed totally with what Henry was saying. If anything, I was now feeling a little embarrassed at how I'd turned such a minor issue into something that was pretty much overshadowing what had otherwise been a fantastic week.

"So, are we in a position to move on?" asked Henry, sensing that he'd put my mind at rest.

"Yes, definitely!" I replied. "I take it we're going to be talking about Level Three of the *5 Levels of Formality* today?" I predicted, confidently.

"We certainly are, and I think you're going to enjoy Level Three," Henry announced cheerfully. "Level Three is what I call *The Development Level*."

Henry took out the sheet of paper that he'd previously used to demonstrate the first two *levels of formality*. He drew another circle around the Level Two circle.

18

Level 3 - The Development Level

"Level Three contains the people in your life that you encounter on a regular basis – but are not close enough to you, relationship-wise, to be included in your first two levels."

"Okay," I said, concentrating intently.

"These are the people that *life puts in your way*. They typically include:

- Local shopkeepers
- Other parents at school
- People you regularly see and acknowledge on your daily activities
- Parents of other children at your child's sports activities
- Neighbours you smile at but don't really speak to

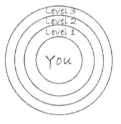

These are people who, although they often make an appearance in your daily and weekly activities, you wouldn't keep in touch with them if your circumstances changed – such as your children moved to a different school or Jamie stopped playing football, for example."

"That makes sense," I nodded. "So, before we became friends, you would have been a Level Three contact of mine?"

"Yes, definitely I would have been. Was I even on your list?" enquired Henry.

"You were, actually. I was planning on stopping you one day and asking you to have a look at my business," I replied.

"And how were you going to do this?" he enquired further.

"By using the script I'd picked up at training, I imagine," I answered.

"The Level Two script?" asked Henry, knowing the answer before he'd even asked the question.

"Yes. The Level Two script. And that would have been wrong because you were a Level Three contact I take it?" I remarked. "So, how should I have approached you?"

"Well, apart from the odd 'Good Morning', we didn't really have much of a relationship to speak of," began Henry. "Your first objective would have been to develop this relationship in a natural, unforced way."

"Okay. So how would I have done that?" I questioned.

"Look, we see each other, pretty much, five mornings per week don't we?" he nodded.

"Yes. School holidays apart, we see each other every weekday," I agreed.

"The best way would be to start off with some small-talk. Comment on the weather or find some common ground – which in our case would be Olivia and Jamie. Over the course of a week, we could have had five 30 second conversations where we had built rapport," Henry explained.

"I see. Then I pitch you with the business on the Friday?" I asked, jumping the gun a little.

"No. Well, possibly yes, but only if the situation was to arise and it felt natural," Henry replied.

"The first thing you have to remember with Level Three is that it is a very *relaxed* and *forgiving* level. And what I mean by that," he went on, "is that the very definition of Level Three affords you time. Time to *develop* relationships and time to *allow* suitable opportunities to arise," he explained.

"So, how exactly do I bring up the subject of what I do?" I asked, intrigued.

"You don't. They do," Henry replied bluntly.

"So, I talk about the weather and the kids until they suddenly ask me about my work?" I probed, still a little unconvinced.

"Kind of. But you skilfully control the situation so they naturally feel that they should ask. You use the power of *Reciprocal Questioning*," Henry went on.

He could see my expression of bemusement, but I was sensing a very steep learning curve approaching.

"Let me put it simply," said Henry. "If I wanted *you* to enquire about *my* health, how could I do that, without even mentioning my health?"

I was a little confused, but I felt that there was a clue in the way that he'd stressed the word 'my'.

Before I could get my thoughts together, Henry went on, "How do people generally greet each other when they meet or speak on the phone?"

"Hello, how are you?" I said.

"And what is the other person's reply, in most cases?" Henry asked.

"I'm fine, how are you?" I answered, not yet realising that I'd stumbled across the simple answer.

"Exactly!" proclaimed Henry. "Do you see what happens there? The first person asks a question that makes the second person feel obliged to return the question."

"Yes. Yes I do. And I'd never really realised that this happened," I said, feeling like the answer was under my nose all along.

"Let's take it another step, using the same technique. How could I make *you* ask *me* where I was going on holiday this year, without mentioning my own holiday to you?" asked Henry.

I paused for a while. I thought about what I'd just discovered and how I could use it to answer Henry's poser.

"I've got it!" I exclaimed. "By asking *me* where *I* was going on *my* holiday."

"Correct!" called out Henry, triumphantly. "That is exactly how I'd do it. I'd ask a question that would, *in most cases*, make you answer, then feel obliged to *reciprocate* with the same question back to me."

"So," he went on, "using *reciprocal questioning*, how would you encourage me to ask you about your business?"

"Easy!" I exclaimed confidently. "I'd ask *you* about *your* business, and you'd feel obliged to ask *me* about *mine*."

"Correct again!" said Henry. "But I must warn you. This doesn't work immediately in 100% of cases. You must be aware that people *absolutely love* talking about themselves. In fact, I've heard it said many times that, 'themselves', is almost everyone's favourite topic. So, be prepared that their *reciprocal question* may take some time to come back at you."

"What, like 20 minutes or something?" I laughed.

"If you're lucky," answered Henry. "Sometimes, it may take several exchanges, perhaps spanning weeks and months, for the question to arrive."

"Oh, I see," I said, losing a little bit of my enthusiasm for *reciprocal questioning*.

"But the beauty of Level Three," assured Henry, "is that you have the *gift of time*. These are people that you get to see regularly. If the situation doesn't lead to you naturally speaking to them about your business this time, then there's always the next time. Just concentrate on building relationships with people, where you speak to each other about your lives, and I can promise you that they will eventually, naturally, ask you what you do."

"Can you see why I like Level Three?" asked Henry.

"I suppose so," I said, not entirely convinced of my own reply.

"Level Three of the *5 Levels of Formality* is where you can *develop* subtle skills that will *develop you* significantly as a person. And it is the level where you can have the most fun," Henry explained.

"Enjoy your conversations with people," he enthused. "Take pleasure in finding out about their lives, what they enjoy, what their dreams are, what they do, where they go and, perhaps most importantly, what their concerns are."

"Why do you say that about their concerns?" I asked.

"Well, their concerns are very often their *hot buttons*," replied Henry. "These are the things that they worry about most and may well be the very reasons why they eventually join your business."

"Like money worries?" I questioned.

"Yes, definitely money worries, but not exclusively. Many people that have plenty of money have very little time. Maybe their *hot button* would be the lack of time they get to spend with their families because of the hours they work," explained Henry.

"But you can only find out these things by making conversation with people and digging a little deeper. In most cases, you'll find that the majority are more than willing to tell you pretty much everything about their lives, given time."

"The more information you can find out about people, the more powerful a position you will be in when they eventually ask you about your business, because this is where the *'you know how most people'* method comes into its own."

"The *'you know how most people'* method'?" I asked. "What's that?"

"It's a technique that I picked up from world-class Network Marketer, Tom 'Big Al' Schreiter. It's a very simple process of using people's *hot buttons* to encourage them to take a look at your business," Henry began to explain.

"Let's say, for example, that you've been building rapport with one of the other parents at the school gate over a period of time, and she's revealed to you that she hasn't taken the family away on holiday for several years due to financial issues. So, you've stored this *hot button* away for future use, because you feel sure your business opportunity could help her."

"Now, let's say that, a week or so later, the time comes when she asks you about what you do for a living. Now you *could* say:

'I sell health products, can I show you all about it?' which may or may not result in the desired outcome.

Or, you could use the *'you know how most people'* technique and say something along the lines of:

"With the current financial climate as it is, you know how most people are having to miss out on taking their families on holiday? Well, I show people how, in just a couple of hours per week, they can build a 2nd income stream that will give them more disposable income to spend on their loved ones."

"I can see how that works," I said. "I've used her *hot button* to describe how I can help her, specifically."

"Yes. And without building rapport beforehand, you'd have no way of knowing what her primary concern was," said Henry. "This is why Level Three is described as the *Development Level*, as much of the success is in the preparation and rapport building."

This was all making a lot of sense to me, but I still needed convincing that I could influence people to ask me about my business 100% of the time.

"This all sounds fantastic Henry, and I can see how it would work, but what happens if you've been speaking to someone for ages, you know, like *months* or even *years*, and they still don't seem to be getting any closer to asking you about your business. Surely there's a way of forcing the issue a little?" I asked, bravely.

"Well, maybe *forcing the issue* is putting it a little strongly, but I understand what you are saying because it does happen. This is where

107

you need to use the knowledge that you've gathered about their *hot buttons* in a different way," Henry explained.

"Great, so how do I do that?" I responded.

"Okay, so let's say that, over the course of a few weeks, you've taken your daughter, Emily, to her swimming lessons and you've struck up some rapport with one of the other fathers. During your conversations you've found out that he feels trapped in his dead-end job because, although the pay isn't great, it covers his mortgage and bills. Obviously, your Network Marketing business would be an option for him if he wanted to make some extra money, part-time," Henry went on.

"It certainly would," I agreed. "So, when he mentions that he's broke, I jump in and tell him that he needs to join my business, do I?"

"Maybe not that forcefully or obviously!" laughed Henry. "This is where you need to use a bit of subtlety. As much as you feel the urge to provide the solution to his problems immediately, the best course of action is to make a mental note of his *hot button* and store it away. You can then use it a little further down the line to control the direction of the conversation."

"I'm intrigued," I responded. "I'm intrigued as to how you'd do that."

"Well, it's quite simple. In this example, you'd choose your time carefully – possibly when you are alone and unlikely to be interrupted, and you'd say something along the lines of:

"Jim, do you know how you were telling me a while ago that you felt that you were trapped in your job because it paid enough to cover your bills, but little else? Well, if I could show you a way, in just a couple of hours per week, that you could build a home-based business that would provide more income and, in 3-5 years, more choices for you, would you be interested in finding out more?"

"I like that!" I said. "So, what if he asks me what it's all about? How do I handle that?"

"With *control* and *posture*. Think about it. If he's asked you what it's about, he basically answered 'yes' to your question. You asked him if he'd be interested in finding out more, and he's just asked you what it's all about – he wants to find out more!" explained Henry.

"I suppose he has, yes," I agreed.

"*Control* means that you take the conversation in the direction of *your* choosing. And *posture* means that you stick to that path *regardless* of what he asks. Like mine, your business has a proven method of demonstrating the opportunity, so, expose him to it on *your* terms – not *his*," said Henry, very directly.

"If the situation allows, then maybe you could show him there and then. But if you'd rather meet at another time, remain in control, keep your posture and make suitable arrangements," Henry instructed.

"Okay, but what if he is persistent in wanting to learn more *immediately* and refuses to meet up at a later date?" I asked, feeling like I was constantly providing hurdles to Henry's solutions.

"Then you take the opportunity away," said Henry, bluntly. "This is *your* business and you know how to best demonstrate it. If he's not willing to view it on your terms, then you withdraw the offer. You don't need to be aggressive. Just a firm recognition that he's not doing it your way will usually do the trick:

"*Okay, well you've obviously not got time to look at this opportunity at the minute and I want to do it justice by showing it you correctly. So let me know when it is fine to get together and I can show you how it works.*"

"Usually, this *taking back* or *withdrawal* of the offer creates a fear of loss and they'll generally agree to do it your way," Henry explained.

"I love that!" I enthused. "So if I keep my posture and refuse to be drawn into demonstrating the opportunity on their terms, I can keep full control of the conversation?"

"Exactly," agreed Henry. "And this is exactly why I love Level Three of the *5 Levels of Formality* so much."

"Now, time is pressing," said Henry, clearing away the coffee mugs. "I need to give you your latest task."

"I'm going away on holiday for 10 days, so it'll be two weeks before we can meet again. But that's fine because it will give you time to work on your Level Three skills."

"What I want you to do is develop ten relationships with people who are on your Level Three list. Some of them, you'll already be quite friendly with. Others, you'll need to begin the relationship from the start. You'll need to develop small-talk about the weather or things that you have in common. But you need to progress your relationship with them so that you can find out more about their lives and their *hot buttons*," Henry explained.

"So," I interrupted, "do you want me to have pitched the business to all ten of them by the time we next meet – in two weeks?"

"No. I'm not really concerned with how many people you've shown your business opportunity to," replied Henry. "The main goal is to develop your skills in building relationships. If, during the course of this exercise, the opportunity to speak about your business naturally arises, then take it, by all means."

"But Level Three of the *5 Levels of Formality* is all about *development* and *rapport building*. When you're a huge success at this business in a few years' time, you'll look back at this skill as the one that was the most beneficial. It will be worth thousands of pounds to you. Take my word for it," Henry assured me.

"Wow! I've learned so much today!" I exclaimed. "I've taken so many notes and I can't wait to start using these Level Three skills with the other parents at school and at the kids' sports activities, as well as my butcher, the lady at the newsagents and our postman."

As I drove away from Henry's home, my mind was furiously trying to make sense of everything that he had just taught me. It would probably need a good review of my notes for it to sink in entirely, but it all made sense at the time, so I was certain these skills would prove valuable to me and my business.

19

Warm Them Up… With Rapport

That evening Zoe wanted to catch up with some television programmes that she had recorded. I never really followed them myself, so I decided to sit in my study and reflect on what I had learned earlier in the day whilst at Henry's and begin to think about how I could start to put it into action.

Level Three, 'The Development Level', I thought to myself. *Who did I know that would be included in this level?*

As I looked down my List, circling those who I considered to be Level Three contacts, I realised that, despite being a fairly sociable person, I was actually a little more private and reserved than I had first appreciated. I was on *nodding and smiling* terms with lots of people but never really made the effort to get into deeper conversations with them. I didn't even know a lot of their names, writing descriptions like 'Luke's Dad' on my list.

It wasn't something I did deliberately, it was just my natural way. In fact, on further reflection, I realised this was how the vast majority of people were. I would have to *open-up* a little more with the people whose paths I crossed on a regular basis and start to make a little more effort to get to know them if I was to begin to uncover their concerns, or *hot buttons*, as Henry described them.

I realised it wasn't going to be too difficult. An image had surfaced in my mind which represented my relationships with the people on Level Three. It was a scale, starting at one end 'Cold' and the opposite end was 'Warm'.

Every person on Level Three was scattered somewhere along this scale, depending upon what I knew about each of them up until this point today. I drew out the scale on a piece of paper and started to write names along it, according to where I thought our relationship was at this moment in time. It occurred to me that, if I transferred this scale, with my prospects' names, onto my whiteboard, I could erase them and move them further along the scale as our relationships became warmer. I eagerly did just that and realised that it made it much easier for me to create a picture in my mind of my Level Three prospects.

I noted that the majority of them sat closer to the 'cold' side of the scale at the moment, some were around the middle, and there were a couple that were closer to the 'warm' side. As I looked at the diagram I had drawn, it made perfect sense that to mention my business opportunity to those that I still deemed 'cold' would feel awkward, out of place, and inappropriate. It would feel easier and more natural to bring it up with those closer to the warmer side of the scale, because I already knew enough about them through past conversations to start to match up my business opportunity with their *hot buttons*.

It dawned on me that my job with Level Three contacts was simply to get to know people more, and, over time, gradually move them from the 'cold' side of the scale across to the 'warm' side, where I would know enough about them to be able to bring up the subject of my business, when the opportunity arose, without any awkwardness.

Although it made perfect sense now, I also understood why Henry was unconcerned about how many people I would actually show my business to over the fortnight break we had between meetings – there simply weren't enough people 'warm' enough at this moment in time to prospect in any significant number.

114

I resolved that the next time each one of my *colder* contacts smiled or acknowledged me in some way, I would take the time to start a conversation instead of simply smiling back. This was going to take some time. I told myself that I wouldn't force anything unnaturally, but I did plan to move the conversations we would have in a direction that would help me discover the information I needed, using the skills Henry had taught me this morning. In fact, there was only one person who I considered to be 'warm' enough to pitch my business to at this moment in time. That was Neil.

Neil was one of the parents from Jamie's football team. I got on well with all of the parents at football and always acknowledged them whilst we were stood watching the games, but Neil was the only one who I had ever spoken further with. We both supported the same professional football team and our conversation had started one night when we both arrived wearing identical scarves.

He had told me in the past that he was a National Account Manager for a large software company. He was clearly well paid, dressed in expensive looking suits and drove a brand-new BMW, which was replaced regularly with the latest model. Thinking back on our past conversations, I also remembered that a few months ago he had mentioned that, although he was doing well at work, he didn't enjoy being away from home as often as he was, and really valued the time he got to watch his son Jake play football. I wondered how I could use this information together with my new knowledge, and resolved that if the opportunity came up naturally, I would attempt to do so when I saw him at the boys' next match on Sunday morning.

20

Red, Red Wine

There was a knock on the door. I opened it and was greeted with the sight of Amy, our next door neighbours' teenage daughter. It was Friday evening and she had arrived to look after Jamie and Emily whilst Zoe and I went to a 40th birthday party. After the usual pleasantries, we kissed our children goodnight and left for a much-needed and all-too-rare night out together.

*   *   *

The party was going great. It was being held at the home of one of Zoe's work colleagues, so I had the opportunity to meet lots of new people. Given that I had resolved to become more sociable, I made a special effort to engage in conversation with those I was introduced to, instead of the usual nod and smile that I would have done in the past.

We had been there for around an hour when the doorbell sounded. I was surprised when someone I recognised walked into the main room. Simon was one of my sister Katie's first boyfriends. I hadn't seen him for a few years, and, although his relationship with my sister had ended, we had all remained friends. I knew he had since married and I'd heard from a mutual friend that he ran a property business.

His face broke into a broad grin when he saw me, and he walked straight across the room, offering his hand for me to shake.

"Great to see you again, Sam!" he exclaimed. "How are you?"

"I'm great, thanks," I replied, shaking his hand firmly. We introduced our wives to each other and began to reminisce about the past.

"How's business?" I asked after a short time. "I understand you're in property?" I decided that I would try out some *reciprocal questioning* at the earliest available opportunity.

"That's right," he replied. "It's going well, although I have a few other business interests too. What are you up to nowadays?" he continued.

Wow, that worked quickly! I thought to myself.

"Well, I'm still working at the same place, full-time, but I've also recently started a part-time business too. In fact," I continued, ***"I'm glad I've bumped into you, Simon. Now isn't the right time to talk, but you clearly understand business. Would you have some time in the near future where I can pop over and see you and show you what I'm doing? I would really value your opinion,"*** I asked.

"Absolutely!" he returned. "Here's my card. Shoot me a text tomorrow and we'll arrange something. I've promised Helen that I won't talk business tonight. Isn't that right?" he asked, glancing at his wife.

"He never shuts up about it!" she said. "So I've made him promise that the conversation is purely social tonight," she laughed.

"That's my fault then, I'm sorry," I said, holding up my hands in a gesture of surrender. We all laughed, and Simon suggested we should grab some more drinks.

As they walked away, Zoe turned and whispered to me. *"Very slick!"* she said.

"What do you mean?" I asked, smiling. It suddenly dawned on me that the skills I had learned from Henry were now coming to me more naturally without much forethought or preparation.

I had subconsciously identified that Simon was a Level Two contact and I had naturally used the appropriate *favour and feedback* technique with him. I had also handled it professionally and with posture too. I afforded myself a little smile and enjoyed the feeling of accomplishment I had. Maybe I *was* getting good at this?

The party continued into the small hours, and as my consumption of red wine increased, so did my confidence around others. I found it much easier to participate in conversations with people I had never met before, and had a lot of fun getting to know them.

I found myself in the kitchen talking to Alan and Dipesh, two of Zoe's work colleagues. I hadn't met either of them before, but we found we had plenty in common. The conversation had so far taken in football, the pedestrianisation of the town centre, our children, and work. We were now discussing our holiday plans for the next year.

"We're going to struggle to get away at all," said Dipesh. "My wife has had her hours reduced at work, so money is a little tight. The best we can hope for is a weekend in my sister's caravan on the coast," he continued glumly.

"We're in a similar position," Alan replied. "We had some money squirreled away for a holiday to Spain, but the head gasket needed replacing on the car and it's wiped us out again."

Filled with confidence from the red wine, I seized my chance. This looked like a perfect opportunity to use the *you know how most people* script.

119

"You know how most people can't afford to go on decent holiday nowadays?" I blurted out.

Alan and Dipesh both looked at me.

"Well, if I could show you a way of earning loads more money working just an hour a week so that you could retire in three years, would you be interested?" I continued.

They looked at each other uneasily, and then Alan spoke.

"Nah, you're alright," he said.

There was an awkward silence.

"You've both just told me you're broke, and I've offered you a way out!" I exclaimed. "You can't be that bothered about having no money if you don't want to take a look at my opportunity."

The awkward silence continued.

Dipesh glanced over my shoulder and waved to his wife, "Isn't it about time to go?" he asked her, nodding his head.

"We'd better be off too," said Alan, shaking my hand. "Nice to meet you," he said, and made his way out of the room. Dipesh followed.

I was suddenly stood alone. Fuelled by a couple of glasses of wine, I had stupidly rushed into pitching my business to two decent prospects, without any consideration for our relationship to each other and had lost all professionalism, control and posture.

Not so slick after all, I thought. I decided it was about time for us to go home too.

21

Back On The Horse

Next morning, I laid in bed staring at the same familiar spot on the ceiling. I needed to get up shortly if I was to get Emily to her swimming class on time, but my thoughts quickly began to reflect on last night's party. A sense of embarrassment welled-up inside me as I recalled how I had completely ruined the chance to develop two relationships by becoming over-excited and talking about my business far too soon. I resolved to be more controlled in the future.

A short while later I was sat, coffee in hand, watching Emily swim. Another parent, Gemma's mother, smiled at me. I smiled back, and having decided to make a bigger effort in getting to know people, and wanting desperately to move on from last night's embarrassing episode, I struck up conversation.

"Morning," I offered.

"Good morning," replied Gemma's mother.

"They're getting really good at this, aren't they?" I said, gesturing towards our children swimming in the pool.

"They are!" exclaimed Gemma's mother. "She absolutely loves coming here and it's good exercise for them too."

"It is," I agreed. "Emily's older brother loves his football, so it's nice that she has an interest in something too. She's even talking about competing at the Olympics!" I enthused.

"Really? Wow!" replied Gemma's mother. "I'm not sure Gemma could go that far, but she certainly loves coming here."

"Yes, either way, it's good for them. It's nice that they get to mix with other kids from different schools in the area too," I said.

"Definitely," agreed Gemma's mother.

"I'm going to get a refill," I said. "Can I get you one?"

"That would be lovely," she replied, holding out her empty cup.

"Back in a minute," I said, standing to return to the café.

I was beginning to enjoy our conversation, and realised that being just a little more sociable wasn't as difficult as I had first imagined. With last night's debacle still fresh in my mind, I reminded myself not to try to force the conversation too quickly. In fact, I decided that I would actually refrain from talking about my business today. Instead I'd simply concentrate on getting to know Gemma's mother a little more.

With fresh coffees in hand, I made my way back to the seating area with no plan other than to enjoy getting to know my new friend a little more.

"Here you go. My name's Sam, by the way," I said, handing her the cup.

"Mine's Linda," she replied, smiling.

I spent the best part of an hour learning more about where Linda and Gemma lived, their horses, and where they liked to go on holiday. With no pressure to 'pitch', I really enjoyed myself.

I spent the afternoon calling my new team members and making sure they were all booked onto their next trainings, and that they would be attending the business opportunity meeting on Tuesday evening. We arranged to meet an hour early to review their progress so far, and I wanted to share some of the new skills I had learned from Henry.

22

"So, what do _you_ do, anyway?"

As usual, Sunday morning was spent stood at the side of a football pitch watching Jamie play.

We had arrived a little early, so in the spirit of getting to know more about people, I helped Jamie's coaches, Darren and Nick, put up the goalposts, corner flags, and hang the nets.

"That is very much appreciated!" said Darren, as I pressed the final corner flag into the ground.

"Many hands make light work," I said. "No problem at all."

"It's amazing how quickly it all gets done when there are more people helping," said Nick. "Trainings are a nightmare during the week with the nights' drawing in. By the time we've got everything set up, there's barely any light left sometimes."

"Would it help if I got Jamie here fifteen minutes early to help set up?" I asked.

"Could you do that?" replied Darren. "It would be a great help to us all if you could."

"I can't promise every time, but I'll try my best," I said. "More often than not I think I can get away from work early enough to do it."

"That would be brilliant, thank you," replied Nick. "My work won't let me leave early, even though they know I'm volunteering," he continued.

"That's a shame," I replied. "What do you do for a living?" I ventured.

"I've been a fireman for 15 years," replied Nick. "It's okay, but the hours are pretty unsociable and it's getting tougher with all of the cutbacks."

"Yes, I saw the news recently," I said, hearing his *hot button* revealing itself but also resisting the urge to offer the obvious solution.

"Only ten more years and I'm done!" said Nick, laughing. "Thanks for your help, I'd better get these lads organised," he said, nodding towards Jamie and the cluster of boys lazily kicking a ball around between them.

I smiled and took my usual place on the touchline. *That's another person that I've moved towards the warmer end of the scale,* I thought to myself.

It was too soon to talk to Nick about my business opportunity at the moment, but I would mentally file away the information he had volunteered and focus on gradually getting to know him more and more until the right time presented itself. On reflection, Level Three was much easier than I had thought, and I could see why Henry enjoyed this level so much.

"How's it going mate?" asked Neil as he took his place beside me on the touchline.

"Good, thanks. What about you?" I returned.

"Great. Nice relaxed weekend for once, I even managed to get to the game for the first time in nearly a year yesterday – did you see it?" he continued.

"I saw the highlights. Looked a bit dull to me," I said.

126

"The sooner we get rid of this coach, the better, if you ask me," said Neil.

We continued to discuss the gradual decline of our football team over the last ten years. Jamie's team took the lead.

"How's work?" I asked.

"Same old, same old," replied Neil, wrinkling his nose.

"What about you? What do you do anyway?" he asked. "I don't think you've ever told me."

I saw my opportunity and composed myself.

"Well, you know how most people have to work long hours nowadays and are often away from their families?" I began, drawing upon the information he had disclosed about himself during previous conversations.

"Uh-huh," replied Neil, stepping back from the touchline to avoid getting embroiled in a particularly hard tackle being played out at our feet. "That certainly describes my life at the minute."

"Well, I show people how, in just a couple of hours per week, they can build a 2nd income that will enable them to cut down on their hours at work and give them more time to spend with their loved ones," I continued.

"Really? How do you do that then?" he asked, shifting his gaze from the football match to me.

Posture and control, I thought to myself.

"It would take me twenty minutes to explain and now isn't really the time, but if you're interested, I'd be happy to meet for a coffee soon and explain what it's all about," I said.

"Okay," replied Neil. "I'm intrigued!"

"Most people are," I replied, "but let's enjoy our weekend and stop this work talk," I said.

"Definitely," said Neil. "Monday morning comes around far too quickly. I'm working from home on Wednesday if you want to meet up?"

"I could spare an hour at lunchtime," I replied, realising that, if I wanted to see Neil soon it would have to be during my lunch hour. "How about we meet at that new coffee shop on the High Street at midday?"

"Perfect," said Neil.

"Go on Jamie!" I shouted, encouraging my son on another of his famed 'mazy runs' and also changing the direction of our conversation at the same time. That felt good!

Wednesday arrived, and over steaming cups of coffee, I once again let the presentation tools do the work for me and recruited another distributor, Neil, into my rapidly-growing team.

23

High Praise, Indeed

It was Thursday morning again and I was on my way over to Henry's house, having had a two week break since our last meeting.

I was very happy with my progress while Henry had been on holiday. I was loving Level Three of The 5 Levels of Formality. It was the least daunting of the levels I'd learnt about so far, and was simply based on engaging people in conversation, which I'd found extremely enjoyable.

I'd signed up just one distributor, Neil, who I'd put at the warm end of the Level Three scale. The process had worked like clockwork, using the techniques I'd picked up from Henry. But I'd also moved a dozen or so relationships along the scale from cold to warm. Henry had asked me to do this with ten people by the time we next met, but I'd found it so natural and without pressure that I'd just taken every opportunity that presented itself.

As ever, Henry was awaiting my arrival and waved through the window of his living room as I drove up along his driveway.

"Long time, no see!" he shouted cheerily as I stepped out of the car.

"Yes, although, to be honest, it's flown by," I responded. "I've been so busy! I've signed up a new distributor and developed relationships with about a dozen more people."

"Okay, okay, let's get into the house before you tell me all about it. You've clearly been working hard on your Level Three prospects. Let

129

me pour the coffee and you can explain everything in detail," laughed Henry. We walked into the house.

"So, this new distributor. Was he or she from your Level Three list of prospects?" he questioned.

"Yes. He was someone who I'd identified as being quite a warm prospect. He's the father of one of my son's friends. We're quite friendly and always chat at the football on a Sunday morning. I already knew his *hot button* - he spent too much time away from his family - so I used *reciprocal questioning* to encourage him to ask me what I did, then the *you know how most people* technique to explain what I do."

Explaining it to Henry in this way highlighted to me just how effectively I'd used the processes that he'd been teaching, and yet Neil hadn't suspected a thing. As far as he was concerned, our coffee meeting just came about through natural conversation at the side of the football pitch.

"Textbook!" approved Henry. "I'm really impressed. Level Three of The 5 Levels of Formality requires application and a willingness to improve your people skills. I couldn't be more pleased with your attitude, Sam."

Wow. I suddenly felt humbled by Henry's words, but it meant a lot to me. Just the thought that Henry was impressed with me was high praise indeed.

"And what about the other nine I tasked you with speaking to?" he asked.

"I've developed relationships with about a dozen people in total," I replied. "I've struck up a chatty relationship with one of the mums at Emily's swimming lessons, but I've not pitched her with my business yet. I see her a few times per week so I'm just indulging in regular conversation with her at the minute – finding out more about her, trying to discover what her *hot buttons* are."

"Terrific," Henry responded. "There's no rush with many Level Three prospects. Just take your time and enjoy finding out more about people through natural conversation. It's a dying art these days when everyone's attention seems to be fixed on some mobile screen or another."

"I've also started to chat to the lady at my local newsagents. I've been a customer for years but other than the daily "Good morning" and "Thank you" when she hands me my change, I've never really spoken to her. I now know her name, what time she gets up each morning and what time she finishes work to go home. We're getting quite familiar now."

I told Henry of other situations where I'd taken the opportunity to develop existing relationships with people during the previous fortnight and, when I shared with him my whiteboard idea, and the fact that I pictured Level Three as a scale from cold to warm, I wasn't quite prepared for his response:

"Wow! I love that concept, Sam," he said. "Do you mind if I use it too? It would really help me keep a track of my Level Three prospects. In fact, I think a few members of my team might benefit from that idea as well."

I was dumbfounded. I'd actually had an idea that Henry thought was so good, he wanted to adopt it himself! I was honoured to say, "Yes, of course!" and I couldn't have been more pleased with myself.

My pride was soon dented when I told Henry of the episode at the party where, fuelled with several glasses of wine, I'd lost my composure and *vomited all over* Dipesh and Alan.

"You're in good company making that mistake, Sam," was his unexpected response. "I did something very similar in my early days in the business. It's easy to get too eager to pitch people, especially when you've had a couple of drinks. It's a fantastic way of getting yourself scrubbed from party invite lists."

"I've discovered that," I replied, sheepishly. "Although, in fairness to myself, before the wine took hold, I did speak to a Level Two prospect who had surprisingly turned up at the party and I'm meeting him for a coffee to present my business to him," I added, in an attempt to save face a little.

"Ah, excellent. It's good to see that, despite me asking you to speak to people on Level Three, you're not abandoning your Level Two prospects," encouraged Henry.

"So, I think we need to make a start on Level Four of the 5 Levels of Formality, don't you?" asked Henry.

"Definitely!" I responded eagerly. "Can't wait."

24

Level 4 - The Opportunist Level

"Level Four is also known as *The Opportunist Level*," he began, taking out the now-familiar diagram and drawing another larger circle around the previous four circles.

"It's called this because much of it isn't really planned, whereas, when using the first three levels, you have an element of control and you can plan your approach ahead. Level Four doesn't afford you that luxury in most cases," he went on. "But that doesn't mean that you can't be prepared for the unexpected."

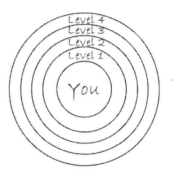

"How do you mean?" I asked. "If I don't know that something is going to happen, how can I prepare for it?"

"By learning how to *warm up* cold relationships in an instant," Henry began to explain.

"Here is a list of the people typically found on Level Four:"

- A tradesman in your home
- A delivery person
- A cashier at a shop that you don't often visit
- A bartender in a pub

"The thing about these people is that, unlike those on Level Three, you don't usually get much time to build rapport or *warm them up*. Here, you have to think on your feet. For example, if you're getting served in a bar, you might only have a minute or so to speak to the barman and get him chatting. Obviously, in this situation, you're not going to get his life story, so you're unlikely to uncover his *hot buttons*," Henry went on.

"So, how do I turn him from a cold prospect into a warm one in that time?" I questioned.

"By *chatting to him* about his job, *complimenting him*, then asking a *direct question* that gauges his interest in your opportunity," was Henry's frank reply.

"I know that sounds a little complicated to start with, but once you've had a bit of practice, it will come much more naturally, as you've found already with the previous three levels," Henry said, assuringly.

"Let's break it down into three parts:"

1. "Talking to them about their job is as simple as:"

    - *Wow, it's busy in here tonight isn't it?*
    - *So, do you just do the evening shift?*
    - *Do you work here full time, then?*
    - *Do you enjoy your job?*

You'll find that a question like any of the above will get them talking and, because the topic is about themselves, they'll naturally warm to you a little," Henry explained.

"Okay, I can see how that would work. But then what do I do?" I asked, eager to find out more.

2. "The second part is to *compliment them*," Henry replied. "Again, keep it simple and, most importantly, *keep it sincere*. Examples would include:"

- *Your personality seems perfect for what you do.*
- *It's always good to be served by someone with a smile on their face.*
- *You really seem to know what you're doing.*
- *So, how long would it take me to get as good as you are at your job?*

"Can you see how we're building rapport and warming them up here? In just a few moments you've asked them a question about their favourite topic, themselves, and you've complimented them on their work. If you're sincere, how can they fail to like you?" Henry reasoned.

"Well, it'd be pretty much impossible wouldn't it?" I agreed. "If somebody said something like that to me, it would make me feel really good."

"Exactly," said Henry, "which tee's up the final part perfectly."

3. "The third and final part is when you gauge their interest with a very direct question," Henry continued. "Again, get a compliment in there as the reason for your approach."

"How do you mean?" I questioned.

"Well, you're going to show them an opportunity and it would be great to let them feel that the reason you're showing it to them is because they've impressed you in some way. So compliments such as:"

- *Look, I really like your manner.*
- *You've looked after me really well today*
- *You've got a great way with people…*

"This prepares them for what comes next, and this is the part that you need to learn *word-for-word*," explained Henry.

"Okay," I said eagerly, leaning forward. "I love a good script."

I readied my pen, in eagerness to take down what was to follow. Henry began.

"I'm a recruiter for my company and we're looking for good people like you. Tell me, if I could show you a way of earning more money, part-time, without affecting your current job, would you be interested in finding out more?"

"Simple as that!" declared Henry. "That little script will work in so many situations. It's so powerful and yet subtle in how it's composed."

"How, exactly?" I asked, still frantically jotting down the script.

"Well, you position yourself as an *authority* when you say, *I'm a recruiter for my company.*" Henry explained. "Then you pay them another compliment, based on what you'd said a few moments earlier when you say *we're looking for good people like you.*"

"I mean, how often does someone say something like that to you? Would it get your attention if they did?" Henry asked.

"It certainly would!" I replied. "It'd make me feel good about myself."

"Exactly. Then, when you ask them the very direct question of *if I could show you a way of earning more money, part-time, without affecting your current job, would you be interested in finding out more?* I think you'd agree that the chances of them wanting to hear more would certainly be increased," Henry explained.

"The question is also very direct and straight to the point. I mean, our role is to find out whether, if we could show someone a way of making more money, part-time, they would be interested in finding out more. So, why not just ask that question straight out? If they decline, then fine. But at least we found out in a very direct, pain-free way, and we can move on to the next prospect."

That makes sense," I agreed. "Why bother composing a slick sales pitch when it is sometimes better to simply ask the question directly? I like that."

"So, let me just run through Level Four again to make sure that I've fully understood," I said.

1. Strike up conversation and ask them a question.
2. Compliment them on how they do their job.
3. Gauge their interest by referring back to the compliment, say that you're a recruiter for your company and are looking for someone like them, then ask them if they'd be interested in knowing more about a part-time opportunity, using your script, *verbatim*.

"Pretty much as simple as that," confirmed Henry. "Obviously, if they agree to take a look, you get their details so that you can provide them with some information. As in the earlier levels, don't be drawn into explaining there and then. Keep that *composure* and *control* of the exchange."

"In each situation, the length of time you'll have to do all of this will vary. For example, the exchange with someone who delivers a parcel to your home may be less than a minute, whereas a guy repairing your washing machine may be there for a couple of hours or more. Again, your own skill level and judgement, as with Level Three, will be key, and you'll improve with practice," Henry explained.

"Makes sense. Totally," I said.

"Okay then, here's your task for this week," said Henry. "I think that, given the skills you've just learnt, you could easily have 10 conversations this week, with people in one-off situations. Take the opportunity to quickly go through the three-step process and get an answer to the question: *if I could show you a way of making more money, part-time, without affecting your current job, would you be interested in finding out more?*"

"Okay, you're on!" I declared, as I took up his challenge for the following seven days. And, with that, we said our goodbyes and I was on my way, out into the world again, armed with more fantastic skills.

25

Recognising Opportunities

It was Friday morning and I was eager to get out of bed.

With Henry's instructions fresh in my mind, I was thinking about where I could create opportunities to trial my latest, Level Four skills. I usually drove straight to work once I had dropped the kids off at school, but, this morning, I decided that I would stop in at a coffee shop about two miles from the office and grab myself an Americano. I'd never been to this particular shop before, but it always looked pretty vibrant when passing, so I imagined it might be a good place to jump straight in and start using my new techniques.

It was a little quieter than I had imagined it would be as I walked through the door. There were four or five people occupying tables and just one person stood at the counter. As I approached, the customer before me collected his drink and his change and walked away. I was a little anxious, but I had Henry's Level Four skills in my armoury and I had confidence that they would work.

"Morning mate, what can I get you?" asked the barista, with a welcoming smile. I caught sight of his name badge pinned to his shirt.

"I'll have a large Americano please, Josh," I replied, returning his smile.

"To go, or would you like to sit in?" he continued.

"To go please, I need to get to work," I answered.

"No problem, we'll have you out of here in no time," Josh said. He turned his head and called over his right shoulder to a young lady further along the counter. "Can you rack me up a large Americano to go please, Stacey? This gentleman is in a bit of a hurry."

"That's just £1.99 please," he said with a smile.

"No problem at all," I said, rooting in my pocket for some coins. "It's really nice to be served by someone who cares about their customers, instead of being treated like cattle," I said.

Josh smiled.

"I've never been in here before, I thought it might be a little busier?" I questioned, handing over my money.

"We're really busy between 7 until around 8.30, but it gets quieter after that until lunch time," he replied, handing me my change. "We used to be busy all day, but since those two coffee chains opened up down the road, we've started to notice things tail off."

"I can imagine," I said. "These worldwide chains make life challenging for smaller businesses, don't they?"

Josh raised his eyebrows in agreement, and nodded his head forlornly.

"Sadly, yes," he replied.

I glanced left and saw that my drink was almost ready. Josh walked over to collect it.

Here was my chance, I thought.

As he slid my drink over the counter, I said,

"Look Josh, you've got a really good way with people. I'm a recruiter for my company and we're looking for good people like you. Tell me, if I could show you a way of earning more money, part-time, without affecting your current job, would you be interested in finding out more?"

He leaned back slightly and raised his eyebrows once more.

"Well...I suppose I would be. Depending on what it was," he replied. "What is it?"

Luckily, I had my wits about me and realised that I shouldn't be drawn into giving any more information at this stage.

"Now's not really the time," I replied. "You're at work and I've got to get to work! Write your number down for me and I'll call you," I continued, sliding a napkin over to his side of the counter.

Josh scribbled his number down.

"Great stuff, I'll be in touch. I'm Sam, by the way," I said, taking back the napkin and slipping it safely into my pocket.

"Have a great day," I said, turning to leave the shop.

"You too," Josh replied as I walked out of the door.

That wasn't so bad, I thought, smiling to myself as I sat in the car.

Although it had taken just a few seconds, it had felt totally comfortable to prospect Josh in that way. I realised it was mainly because of the fast rapport building and compliments I had included in our short exchange. I was excited to have a prospect to follow-up with tonight when I got home. I glanced in the rear view mirror before continuing my journey to work.

141

*   *   *

I tried Josh's number six times that evening, without success.

The call just rang out and didn't even go to voicemail. In an age when everyone was almost addicted to their mobile phones, I suspected that he was screening his calls, avoiding me and refusing to answer the phone. I also sent him two texts, reminding him of our conversation earlier in the day.

In the past, I would have been devastated, but my association with Henry and the skills and mind-set he'd instilled into me meant I took this apparent rejection in my stride. After all, it was just *part of the process*. I thought more deeply about what was happening and had a further insight.

Perhaps it wasn't such a good idea to call someone six times in short succession, then follow it with a burst of text messages! I thought.

I pictured Henry talking about *posture* and *composure*. I realised that calling someone incessantly in this way did not look good. In fact, it looked *needy* - another word that Henry had used in our conversations. I felt slightly embarrassed as this dawned on me and I resolved not to do it again.

I went to bed.

*   *   *

As usual, Saturday morning was spent in a blur trying to combine getting Emily to swimming, playing computer games with Jamie, and staying a little longer in bed. It was 9.30 am and we were almost ready to leave for the pool.

Zoe, Emily, and Jamie were already waiting in the car as I grabbed my coat. The doorbell sounded.

I opened the door and was greeted with the sight of a lady holding a parcel.

"Morning!" she chirped. "Number 7?"

"We are," I replied, smiling.

I quickly gathered my thoughts as well as the parcel being offered to me, and composed myself, realising that an opportunity to practise the Level Four skills may be about to materialise.

"Could you sign there for me please?" the lady continued, handing over an electronic device.

"You're bright and cheerful this morning," I ventured. "Not like the usual guys we have around, I barely get a grunt from them."

"That's just me," she replied smiling. "I always look on the bright side."

"I bet you're *mega-busy*, aren't you?" I continued.

"I'm always busy!" she laughed. I laughed too.

"It's refreshing to see that you enjoy what you do though," I continued.

"Thanks. It's okay in this weather, but as soon as the snow and ice arrives, it's not so much fun," she replied.

"I'll bet," I returned. I hesitated to hand back the electronic device.

"Look, I really like your manner. I'm a recruiter for my company and we're looking for good people like you. If I could show you a

way of earning more money, part-time, without affecting your current job, would you be interested in finding out more?"

She tilted her head to one side slightly.

"I could be. Doing what?" she replied.

Again, the coaching from Henry took over.

"Now's not really the time," I replied, nodding towards my car. "You're working, and I've got to get my daughter to her swimming lesson. Write your number down for me and I'll call you at a better time," I continued.

"I usually finish around 4 on a Saturday," she said, handing me a slip of paper.

"If I call you at 5, would you have a few minutes to chat?" I asked.

"That would be perfect. I'm curious!" she laughed.

"We'll speak later," I confirmed. "Now, I've really got to go or we'll be late," I continued, stepping out of the house and turning to lock the door. "Enjoy the rest of your day."

"You too," she replied, making her way back to her delivery van.

"What was all that about?" asked Zoe, as I got into the car.

"Just another business prospect," I replied, smiling. I fastened my seatbelt and started the engine.

*   *   *

It was 5pm and, as agreed, I called the delivery lady.

It went to voicemail. 'Angela's' voice instructed me to leave a message and said she would get back to me as soon as possible. At least I had found out her name. Remembering my experience from last night, I ended the call without leaving a message.

"Another disappointment," I thought.

Henry had warned me that these Level Four encounters were purely *opportunistic*, and, when asking such an unexpected and direct question within such a small timeframe in which to build rapport, I shouldn't expect a high level of success. I was truly beginning to understand that the further away, or colder, a person was in terms of our relationship, not only were differing approaches required, the chances of success diminished too. Despite this, I resolved to keep trying out my skills.

Typically, my phone rang as we sat down to dinner. In our family, we have a rule that we always eat together whenever we can and, when we do, there are to be no electronic distractions around. I let it go to voicemail and continued to eat.

The phone beeped twice to indicate that I'd received a voice message.

I secretly hoped that it was Angela returning my call. It took immense willpower to prevent me from leaving the table to check my phone, but our family rule was cast in stone, so I resisted.

As Zoe cleared away the dirty pots, I pressed the button to retrieve my message.

"Hi, it's Angela, the delivery driver," she said. "I think you might be the man at Number 7. If it is, I'm really sorry I missed your call, we had to work late again tonight. If you're around, please give me a call back."

I smiled to myself as I scrolled up through the recent numbers and redialled. Her message sounded promising.

"Angela, it's Sam. We met this morning and I'm just returning your call," I said breezily.

Henry's advice about *posture, neediness* and *composure* was at the forefront of my mind, so I wanted to sound relaxed about the call.

"Hi. Thanks for calling me back," she replied, in the familiar chirpy way that she had spoken this morning. "I'm so sorry I missed your call, we had a mad rush again at the end of the day and ended up working late."

"No problem at all," I said, not wanting to sound too eager.

Aiming to build further rapport and discover more about her, I asked, "That must be a nightmare at the weekend. Does that happen often?"

"Too often," she sneered. The chirpiness had gone from her voice. "It causes all sorts of problems with my ex-partner and our children. We split up a year ago, and I'm just about back on my feet again," she continued.

She had volunteered some personal information, which was a good sign, but I felt it wasn't really my place to discuss her private life, so I quickly redirected the subject to our earlier conversation.

"I understand, sounds tricky," I said. "So, about our conversation this morning – you said you might be interested in earning more money. This may or may not be for you. That's for you to decide. And I certainly don't want to waste your time, so would it be okay if I sent you a link to a short video which explains what we do? Once you've watched it, you can tell me whether you would like to know more."

"Yes, absolutely," replied Angela.

"Great. What's your best email address?" I asked. I jotted it down.

146

"Thanks," I said. "If I send the link to you now, how soon can you watch it?"

"I'll watch it immediately," Angela answered, enthusiastically.

"Okay, so if I call you again in 10 minutes, you will have watched it?" I replied.

"Definitely," she said.

"The email is on its way now, I'll call again in 10 minutes and you can let me know how interested you are," I said, preparing to finish the call.

"Superb," replied Angela. "I'll watch it right now."

I decided to make a cup of tea to fill the time before I called her again. I tried to remain calm as I watched the clock, but, as always, when someone showed some interest in the business, I felt a mixture of excitement and nervousness. Before I knew it, it was time to call.

"Hi Angela, it's Sam," I said. "Did you watch the video?"

"I did," she replied.

"Great. So, how interested are you in joining us as a business partner?" I questioned.

"It looks really good," she answered. "I've already thought of loads of people who would be interested in the products, and some who would do the business," she said. "But, can you really make that kind of money?"

"Certainly, with time and consistent effort you can," I replied. "Is that your only concern?"

147

"Yes, it just seems too good to be true," she laughed.

"Fantastic!" I replied. "I love it when people say that, it means that they've understood the full potential of the opportunity," I reassured.

"Listen," I continued, "before you decide to come on board, I must stress that, as good as it looks, this is *work* and it takes *time* and *effort*."

"I understand," replied Angela. "I realise that it's not a *get rich quick* scheme."

"Okay, if you've no other concerns, would you like to give it a go?" I ventured.

"Yes, I think I would!" she replied.

"Great. So, what's stopping you registering with us tonight?" I asked.

"Nothing, I suppose," offered Angela.

"Are you in front of your computer now?" I asked.

"Yes," she replied.

"In that case, click the link at the end of the video and you can get registered. I'll walk you through it..." I began.

Five minutes later, Angela was registered and booked onto her first training. I ended the call and smiled inwardly to myself. I was quite proud of how I had handled the conversation, and I had another new team member on board too.

I found that, not only was I becoming adept at using the principles and scripts of the 5 Levels of Formality, I was also using effective lines and phrases that I had picked up from Henry during our general conversations.

"You're getting good at this," smiled Zoe, as she handed me a glass of wine.

I smiled back. "I'm getting there," I said.

*　　　*　　　*

The rest of the week passed without any more distributors joining.

I felt disappointed, but I was learning constantly and certainly getting more and more comfortable with the Level Four principles and skills. As I drove to see Henry, I reflected on my progress over the past week.

On Tuesday I had stopped by a local sandwich shop whilst I ran some errands over my lunch hour. Just as I had done in the coffee shop previously, I'd developed some fast rapport with the lady serving me.

"Listen, I'm a recruiter for my company and we're looking for good people like you. If I could show you a way of earning more money, part-time, without affecting your current job, would you be interested in finding out more?" I ventured.

"No thanks," she replied, cheerily. "I haven't got time for anything else."

"Yes, but…as I said…it won't interfere with your job here," I pressed.

"No, I'm not interested," she said, shutting the conversation down politely, but firmly. "Thanks anyway."

I collected my lunch and left, dejected.

I began to wonder why the script had failed to work despite having delivered it word for word, as Henry had instructed. Some doubt had begun to creep in. In total, I had managed to prospect 10 people as Henry had challenged, and I found that many people were simply not interested in looking at the business opportunity. A handful were, but wouldn't disclose their contact details.

Of those that were interested in looking and were prepared to give their contact information, the majority of them would not answer their phone, and those that did had changed their mind as their interest had waned.

As well as a new team member in the shape of Angela, I had one more person interested. I'd stopped to fill my car with fuel late one night and had engaged the cashier, Charlie, in conversation, managing to pique his interest. He had gone as far as watching the video but had decided he wanted to think about it. I wasn't pinning much hope on him joining, if the truth be told.

I turned into Henry's street once again.

26

Introducing: Helium Balloons

"So, how has your week been?" asked Henry, putting his coffee down onto the table.

"Mmm, a bit up and down, if I'm honest," I replied. "I've enjoyed working with my new team members and I've begun to teach them all about the 5 Levels of Formality. They've certainly had more success in getting appointments with people than I had before I met you."

"Glad to hear it, and well done on duplicating these techniques through your team. Once your team members start to teach them to their team members as well, you'll have achieved some fantastic *duplication* – and that is at the heart of a solid Network Marketing business," Henry responded.

"So, what about the Level Four techniques we covered last week? Have you put them into practice and created opportunities to prospect people?"

"Yes, I've offered the business opportunity to ten people, as you instructed me to do," I replied.

"And what sort of response have you had?" Henry probed.

"Well, I signed up the parcel delivery lady by engaging her in conversation and using the *three-step process* that you taught me. I complimented her on her cheery personality, built some further rapport by asking her about her job, then asked her if she'd be interested in looking at the business opportunity, using your script, word-for-word," I explained.

"Wow! I'm seriously impressed," exclaimed Henry. "A Level Four success in your first week of trying. You must be delighted with yourself."

"Well, I suppose," I replied, rather sheepishly. "But, it's not all been plain sailing."

"Tell me more," said Henry.

"Out of the other nine people, I've got one person who's showing an interest, Charlie, who works at the fuel station. But I've had a mixture of people not being interested, refusing to answer their phones, despite having agreed a time to call, and one lady, who I thought would be perfect for the business, not even agreeing to take a look. That failed attempt spoiled my afternoon, if I'm honest," I declared, reliving the feelings of rejection that I'd experienced a few short days ago.

Henry chuckled and nodded his head. I was struggling to see what he'd found so amusing and took slight offence at him laughing at my misfortune.

"Sam," he began, "you've made some great steps over the last few weeks, but I can see that we still need to work on your mind-set a little."

"What do you mean by that?" I asked, still a little insulted by his attitude.

"Well, let's listen to your language. You told me about a *failed attempt* to get a particular lady to join your business, didn't you?"

"Yes. She didn't even want to look at it. To be honest," I began, bravely, fuelled by my grumpiness at Henry, "you've taught me some great techniques lately, but I'm not so convinced by your Level Four scripts. They don't seem to be as successful as the first three."

Henry chuckled once more. I'd secretly hoped that he'd have been a little offended at my criticism of his teachings. But no. Typically, he remained calm, collected and completely in control of his emotions. Looking back, this exchange had really demonstrated how far I had to go, emotionally, to be on the same level as Henry.

"Sam. If you've failed to get someone to join, then that means that you've tried to get her to join, doesn't it? Does that make sense?" he began.

"Yes, of course. Aren't we all trying to get people to join our business? Surely, that's the whole point, isn't it?" I replied.

"No, not exactly," Henry came back. "We're looking to build a business by finding people who are interested."

"Er…okay," I responded. I was experiencing the familiar feeling that I'd become accustomed to in my meetings with Henry. I wasn't entirely certain of what he was saying, but I was sure an explanation was on its way.

"May I offer you an analogy?" Henry enquired.

"Of course, if it helps you to explain," I replied.

"Okay, well, I've always thought that this business would be much easier if everyone was forced, by law, to carry a helium balloon around with them – a green one if they were interested in looking at a 2nd income opportunity, and a red one if not," Henry began… somewhat surprisingly.

"What do you mean?" I questioned, a part of me wondering whether something stronger had been slipped into Henry's coffee.

"Well, think about it," he went on. "You'd be able to go about your daily business, and instantly see who was and who wasn't interested in your part-time opportunity. It'd save a lot of wasted time and a lot of frustration through rejection. Don't you agree?"

"I suppose," I replied, humouring Henry a little.

"You'd be able to approach the people with the green balloons and not bother with the people carrying the red ones. How simple would that be?" Henry continued. "Unfortunately, that law hasn't been passed and, let's be honest, it's unlikely to ever be passed. Nonetheless, it would be useful for us to imagine that everyone is carrying an invisible balloon, and the only way you can find out whether it's red or green is by asking them a question – the very question that you've been asking people throughout the last week."

"Okay," I said, finally starting to grasp the concept of Henry's off-the-wall analogy.

"You see," Henry went on, "the idea is not to change the colour of people's balloon, it's simply to find out which colour they already are. Some people are interested at this moment in time and some are not, and the only way to find that out, in the real world, is to ask them. This week, you've asked ten people, *if you could show them another way of making more money part time, would they be interested in looking at it*. Is that correct?"

"Yes. Yes it is," I admitted.

"And you've had ten responses to that question haven't you?" he pressed further.

154

"Yes, I've had ten responses," I conceded again.

"So, rather than having *failed*, as you put it a minute ago, you've actually succeeded. You've found out whether they're interested. You've discovered which colour balloon they are carrying and that's all your role entails."

As ever, Henry was making complete sense.

"Rather than seeing someone rejecting the chance to look at the opportunity as a failure on my part, I should see it as a result. I've found out whether they're interested in looking at a part-time opportunity or not? Or, as you put it, I've found out which colour balloon they're carrying!" I said.

"Exactly," replied Henry, "and thank you for humouring my analogy!"

"That's the whole thing about Level Four of the 5 Levels of Formality, Sam," Henry went on. **"The people you are speaking to are strangers and you only have a very limited period of time to build rapport. As a result, people find it easier to ignore your calls or just refuse your offer out of hand. That's just the way it is, but that's not to say that you shouldn't prospect people. You never know, the next person you offer the opportunity to might be your next superstar, so, you might as well."**

Suddenly, I wasn't feeling so deflated about my *failures* and I could see that Level Four was always going to be this way. All it needed was a change in my reaction to those carrying red balloons.

27

Level 5 - The Chicken List

"So," said Henry. "Let's talk about the fifth and final Level of Formality."

"Yes, let's," I replied.

"Do you have your list to hand, Sam?" he asked.

"Yes, it's here. I always carry it with me," I replied.

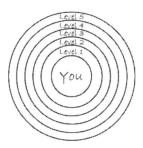

"Just take a look down that list. Who's left on there? Who's not yet been placed into one of the previous four Levels of Formality?" Henry queried.

"Let's take a look. Well, there's Colin, my old boss, the headteacher at the kids' school, Chris, the policeman, who lives a few doors down from me, my local councillor, that guy who works at the local business centre who seems to have quite a few successful businesses..." I said, reeling off the final few remaining people on my list.

"As I thought," Henry interrupted. "Do you see any common thread with these people?"

"Not really," I replied.

"Okay. Well answer me this question honestly," Henry went on. "Why haven't you approached these people yet?"

"Erm, I'm not entirely sure," I said.

Which wasn't the whole truth. Subconsciously, I knew that I'd avoided approaching these remaining people because I was slightly intimidated by them and their success. I felt they would think that Network Marketing was *beneath them* in some way, inviting ridicule and subsequent embarrassment.

"Could it be that these people hold *positions of power*? Could it be that you have subconsciously *put them on a pedestal*? Could it be that you're a little more apprehensive about approaching these types of people?" Henry quizzed.

"Well, thinking about it, you might be onto something," I conceded. "Yes, I'm not entirely comfortable with offering them my opportunity because I'm not sure whether they would need it. If I'm honest, the thought of it scares me a little," I confessed.

"Thought so," said Henry, smiling. "It's nothing to be ashamed of. We've all got a *Chicken List* – people who we delay approaching!"

"Ha ha! *Chicken List*. I like that," I laughed. Then something suddenly occurred to me.

"You. You were a Level Five prospect," I began. "A few weeks ago I had you down as a Level Three, if you remember?"

"Yes," replied Henry. "We did say that I was Level Three because we were acquaintances whose paths crossed daily, so you would have the chance to develop our relationship over time."

"Yes," I replied, "but, actually I subconsciously avoided prospecting you because I was slightly intimidated by your successful persona."

Henry laughed.

"That's interesting to know. I'll take that as a compliment," he replied, visibly embarrassed.

"Okay," I said, quickly moving the conversation along to avoid further embarrassment for either of us.

"How do I *pluck* up the courage to speak to people on my *chicken list*?"

"You don't," replied Henry, completely failing to acknowledge my clever pun. "Someone else does it for you."

"Okay. Are you offering to contact these people on my behalf, Henry? That'd be fantastic of you. I'd love that," I enthused.

"No, no, no!" Henry laughed. "I've really enjoyed helping you out, Sam, but I draw the line at prospecting for you. I've got my own business to build, after all!"

"So, who contacts them?" I questioned.

"A leader from your upline," was Henry's short answer.

"Barney? You want me to get Barney to contact them? He's not even in the business anymore!" I said, a little confused at Henry's suggestion.

"No, I said a *leader* from your upline. Barney, as much as you love him as a friend, isn't a leader. Tell me, who else do you know from your upline?" questioned Henry.

"Nobody really," I said. "Other than Barney, there's nobody I really know that well. There's a fella, Richard, who has called me a couple of times. He called me when I first joined the business, then again when I signed up my first distributor and, I think, every time I've introduced a new team member since."

"And have you ever met him?" enquired Henry.

"No, he's offered to meet me for a coffee, and he says he's always there if I need him, but I've got you as my mentor, so I've pretty much declined his services," I explained.

"Well, he sounds like a leader to me," said Henry. "The frequency of his calls to congratulate and encourage you, the offer to help you... I think this Richard fella might be your man. Tell me, his surname isn't McClaren is it?"

"Er... yes, I think it might be," I replied, quite surprised. "Do you know him?"

"Yes, I've known him for years. He's making some serious money in your business and is a top, top leader. If I was you, I'd make contact with him and take him up on his offer of help," suggested Henry.

"So, you want me to contact him and ask him to contact people from my *chicken list*?" I questioned, tentatively.

"I certainly do. I think it's a fantastic idea," was Henry's instant retort. "And what's more, he'd be absolutely delighted to help. Trust me, I know Richard, and there's nothing more he'd rather do."

"Really? I just contact him out of the blue and ask him to do this? Isn't that a little bit forward?" I questioned, still unsure of Henry's suggestion.

"Yes, without question," Henry affirmed. "Look, Richard McLaren is an excellent Network Marketer and a true leader. I like to think of myself as a half-decent leader as well, and I'd love more people in my team to contact me about helping them. Sadly, we offer our services freely, but very few people actually take us up on that offer. I know that when someone in my team requires my help in contacting people from their list, I jump at the chance."

This concept was quite difficult for me to grasp. Richard McLaren was a virtual stranger to me and I'd not really given him much encouragement when he'd offered to help me out on numerous occasions. Going back to him now and taking him up on that offer made me quite uncomfortable.

"So, that's your task for this week," announced Henry. "Contact Richard about helping you with your chicken list."

"You mean you want me to call him and say, *Hi Richard, it's Sam from your team. I've got some people on my list who I'm a little scared of prospecting. Would you like to approach them from me, please?*" I asked, with a hint of disbelief in my voice.

"Yes, you're getting good at this. That'd be a perfect script!" was Henry's response. "He'll take the names from you and use the tried and tested *third party script* – I'd put money on it."

Recognising a pattern that had emerged over the previous month or so, I said, "Go on then. What's the *third party script*?"

"Well," began Henry, "Richard simply calls your contacts and uses a simple framework. Did you say one of them was called Colin?"

"Yes, Colin was my boss a few years ago. He's really outgoing and I think he'd make a fantastic distributor," I replied.

"Okay then, it'd go like this," Henry explained:

Richard: "Hi, is that Colin?"

Colin: "Yes."

Richard: "Hi Colin, my name is Richard McLaren. You don't know me, but I believe we have a mutual friend in Sam Hirst. He used to work for you?"

Colin: "Yes, that's right. How is Sam? Is he okay?"

Richard: "Don't worry, he's absolutely fine. Colin, the reason I'm ringing you is that Sam and I have recently gone into business together and your name came up in conversation as being a smart, ambitious, motivated type of person. Would that be correct?"

Colin: "Well, yes, I'd like to think so."

Richard: "Fantastic. Well, at the moment we're simply letting people know about our new business and asking their opinion of it. If I got some information over to you would be prepared to look at it, as a favour to Sam?"

Colin: "Yes, of course I'd do that for Sam. It'd be a pleasure!"

Richard: "Tremendous, thank you. What's your best email address?"

Colin: "colin@..."

Richard: "Thank you. I've just sent over some information, it should take you around ten minutes to browse through it. How soon will you be able to look at it?"

Colin: "I'll get a look at it this evening."

Richard: "So, if I call you back at the same time tomorrow morning, you will have looked at it, and you will be able to give me your opinion on it?"

Colin: "Yes, that would be fine."

"And that would be that," said Henry. "You've got your information in front of someone and you've done nothing other than hand your list to Richard.

I left Henry's house shortly afterwards. I was feeling extremely nervous about contacting Richard, having spurned his kind offers previously. But Henry seemed convinced that it would be fine. I decided that I'd give him a call this evening.

28

Unnecessary Reluctance

As the call connected, I cleared my throat ready to speak.

"Hi, Richard McLaren speaking…" said the familiar voice.

"Hi Richard, it's Sam Hirst. I'm in your downline, we spoke a few days ago?" I ventured.

"Hi Sam, how are you?" he replied. "It's good to hear from you again; what can I do for you, Sam?"

"Well, it's a bit of a strange request really," I began. "I've been speaking with one of the parents from my eldest son's class, and it turns out that he knows you. His name is Henry Peters?"

"Ah, yes, I know Henry very well," replied Richard. "We go back years! He's a great guy, and one of the best networkers in the country. I hope he only said nice things about me?" he laughed.

"He did, he did!" I said, laughing in return and warming to the conversation.

"You won't turn Henry's head, if that's what you were hoping," asked Richard. "Like me, he's been with his company for years and built a very large business."

"No, it's not like that at all," I replied. "We got talking one day and after discovering I was just getting started, he kindly offered to coach me. He's already explained about cross-pitching, being a professional, and staying loyal to one network. He's been really helpful, even though he doesn't stand to benefit from it in any way. I can't thank him enough."

"That's Henry, completely selfless and just looking to serve others," replied Richard. "Actually, that explains a lot about your recent success, Sam. If I was a gambling man, I would wager he's been coaching you on the 5 Levels of Formality?"

"Wow, is it that obvious?" I laughed.

"Henry is renowned across the profession for coaching those skills through his company, and I've seen him teach it from the stage at quite a few large Network Marketing events. It's always very well received," continued Richard. "It's very effective and has helped many new starters, like yourself, make sense of their list and educate them in approaching people in the most effective way. He even does regular workshops to allow people to practise in a safe environment, they're incredibly popular and always oversubscribed."

"It's certainly been of huge benefit to me," I responded.

"And now I'm armed with the knowledge that you've been exposed to the 5 Levels of Formality, my second wager would be that you're contacting me for help with the people on Level Five, or your *chicken list*?" quizzed Richard.

I laughed. "Nothing gets past you, does it?" I exclaimed.

Richard chuckled. "Do you want to ask me the question then?"

"Seems a little pointless given you know why I'm calling, but I may as well. *Richard, I've got some people on my list who I'm a little anxious of prospecting. Would you like to approach them for me, please?*" I asked.

"It would be my pleasure," he returned. "No point in wasting time, Sam. Bring your contact list around to my house tomorrow night and we'll make the calls. Here's my address…"

29

Upline Masterclass

As I suspected, Richard lived in the nicer part of town, too. His house was similar to Henry's; clearly expensive and tasteful. To someone who didn't know about the Network Marketing profession it would look like it belonged to a barrister or successful company director. Richard sat opposite me in his home office, a beautiful antique desk between us.

"Might as well do these calls on speakerphone so you can hear them and we can treat this as a training opportunity too," said Richard.

"Sounds good to me," I said. "There are only eight names left on my list."

"For now," Richard replied.

"For now?" I repeated.

"Yes, a fundamental skill is to constantly be adding names to your contact list," he replied. "That way, we never run out of people to speak with. New prospects are the lifeblood of any Network Marketing business."

"That makes sense," I said.

"Okay. Who's first?" said Richard, running his finger down the list and picking up his phone, ready to dial...

For the next 20 minutes I was treated to a masterclass in relaxed and effortless telephone prospecting. Richard used the script that Henry had shared with me, verbatim, handling the calls with ease and securing their agreement to take a look at some information we would be sending over by email.

Each person Richard called treated him like a peer; a fellow 'successful' person. I could clearly see why this was the best way of speaking with those people on Level Five as it took me, and my *self-imposed preconceptions that I had imagined my Level Five contacts might have against me,* out of the equation.

Richard concluded the final call in the same way he had concluded the previous seven calls:

"If I sent you the link over now, how soon could you watch it, Colin?" *he questioned my former boss.*

"I can watch it straight away," replied Colin.

"Great, so if I call you back in 15 minutes, you will have watched it?" Richard probed.

"If it's just a six minute film, then definitely," came the reply.

"Great, I'll call you in 15 minutes," said Richard. "Nice to speak with you."

"It's in the lap of the gods now, Sam," he proclaimed. "Who knows where these people are in their lives, and whether they see our opportunity or not. We've won though – *the success is in the show not the sign-up.*"

I smiled at this newfound wisdom and felt a strange kind of calm as this new knowledge embedded itself in my mind.

"Let me get some more coffee and biscuits and then we'll make the follow-up calls," Richard said.

Once again, I witnessed Richard making simple, measured, and relaxed follow-up calls. Due to the professional and business-like manner in which he conducted them, no-one had dismissed us outright, and it seemed that most of my Level Five contacts had a high degree of interest or at least *curiosity* in our business opportunity.

Richard deftly answered any questions that were asked of him and he either invited them to our next business opportunity open evening or arranged for the three of us to meet and discuss things further over coffee. The free space in my diary for the week ahead began to fill-up, and the sense of anticipation and excitement at the thought of further success expanded in me too.

The future was starting to look ever more bright.

30

Flying The Nest

As I made the, now familiar, drive to Henry's house for our weekly meeting, I reflected on the past seven days. I'd left Henry a week ago, charged with contacting my upline, Richard McLaren, to ask for his help in contacting the final few people on my list – the people on my *chicken list*.

As Henry had predicted with absolute confidence, Richard had been extremely receptive to my request and was using the *third party script* in conversations with my contacts within 24 hours of me approaching him.

Looking back, I was staggered at how well the calls had gone. Each of the eight people that he'd contacted had agreed to take a look at the information; three of them thanked him, but declined any further information, two had agreed to attend an upcoming presentation evening and the remaining three had agreed to meet the two of us for a coffee, where I'd shown them my money presentation and one of them agreed to join as a distributor. The other two, whilst impressed with the business model, decided not to join, but they agreed to let me keep them updated on developments within the company, so they went onto my *No-For-Now List*.

*　　　*　　　*

Handing me my coffee in what had now become *my* mug, Henry nodded with satisfaction as I told him of my progress during the previous seven days.

"To be honest, Sam, I expected nothing less. Richard is extremely professional and confident and, using the *third party script*, only the

173

most closed-minded of people would refuse to take a look at your business," said Henry.

There was a pause. Henry smiled a smile of satisfaction and said, "Wow. What a journey you've been on this last six weeks, Sam. You're a totally different person from the man who approached me at school such a short time ago."

"I certainly am!" I enthused, with pride.

"You know, I'm going to miss these meetings each week. I've really enjoyed your company and your willingness to learn the 5 Levels of Formality," Henry sighed.

Suddenly, I realised what Henry was inferring. His language was politely indicating that his work with me was now done and he felt that I was ready to *go alone* with my business. Although it had only just occurred to me that our meetings were drawing to a close, I tried not to look surprised or disappointed.

"I don't know how I'm ever going to be able to thank you enough, Henry," I said. "I seriously don't know if I'd still be in the business without your help."

"The best way to thank me would be to duplicate what I've taught you throughout your business," said Henry. "You've now got quite a few team members and many of them will be going through the same frustrations that you experienced just a few weeks ago."

"Don't worry about that," I assured Henry. "I'm already teaching the 5 Levels of Formality within my team. I've realised how crucial the first few weeks in the business are so I'm passing on the techniques within days of them joining."

We chatted for a while longer and said our goodbyes. It was quite a sad moment on my part, but at least I had the comfort of knowing that I'd bump into Henry each day at school when I'd be able to pick his brains, if required.

As I drove home, I couldn't help but start to think about the journey I had been on over the past six weeks. As I thought more deeply, I felt the urge to stop the car and take a walk by a local lake. Standing by the water's edge, I could see my reflection in the mirror-like surface. The man staring back at me looked the same as he did six weeks ago, but inside there had been some major changes. He was no longer the frustrated and directionless person that was just starting out in Network Marketing. He was now more focussed, measured, and professional, with a clear track to run on.

I took a deep breath and reflected upon how frustrated I'd been before I met Henry, and how I'd made a complete mess of speaking to my *Level One contacts*, as I now knew them.

I cringed when I recalled how I'd procrastinated about calling people from my list and how I'd worked myself up *trying* to get people to join my business.

This early *failure* had misguidedly driven me to the *cold market* before I'd contacted even a tenth of the people on my warm list.

Using Henry's techniques, I'd not only signed up plenty of customers and recruited quite a few team members, I'd also changed as a person. No longer did I *beat myself up* if someone declined my offer. As Henry had put it, my role was simply to find out which colour balloon people were carrying!

I was also developing as a leader. I was teaching the 5 Levels of Formality to my team and they were benefiting by getting off to a much more positive start than I'd personally experienced, prior to meeting Henry.

I really felt that I'd arrived in Network Marketing and I couldn't have been more excited about the future.

Epilogue

The five years since meeting Henry have simply flown by.

The loud applause shook me out of my daydreaming, and I joined in with the clapping enthusiastically as Henry's daughter, Olivia, walked up onto the school hall stage to receive her Outstanding Achievement award. Henry stood to applaud. My own son, Jamie, sat by the side of the stage, ready to receive his award too. The fact that their respective parents were on a constant journey of personal development, which went hand in hand with building a successful Network Marketing business, was no coincidence. It had clearly rubbed off onto the children too and had resulted in positive, well-rounded young adults. Their attitudes were far beyond their years.

The time had passed quickly and our children were now leaving school. Henry smiled at me as he sat down again. We had become good friends over the years. I smiled back and began to reflect upon how our lives had changed for the better, and also how much I had discovered about myself, all because of a chance conversation in the school yard one morning a few short years ago. Little did I know how significant that would be at the time.

My Network Marketing business had grown steadily and I had been able to significantly reduce the hours I worked in my day job until I was able to walk away from it altogether. I still stayed in touch with my workmates, and, if truth be told, I left with a heavy heart. I wasn't one of those that loathed their *9 to 5*, but I had the opportunity to spend more time with my family, so I seized it.

We had moved house a few months ago into a larger property in a quieter part of town, and, at the same time, Zoe had chosen to give up her job too. She now volunteered three mornings a week, helping out at the local primary school.

We had upgraded the cars as well as the house, and the family holidays we took were now a little more exotic. I found that it was *quality of life* and *experiences* that really mattered to me and I actually wasn't as materialistic as I'd imagined I would be. It was difficult to put a value on the peace of mind I had, knowing everything was covered financially and we would be okay, whatever life threw at us.

Of course, not everyone I recruited in those early days was still with me, although a lot were. Some had fallen by the wayside, and some had become distracted and life had got in the way as often happens, but my business was strong, secure, and still growing. In particular, our close friend, Becky, and Neil, one of the football dads, had built flourishing businesses with incomes to match. Becky was now married with a daughter. Her part-time Network Marketing business had enabled her to choose not to return to work after the birth of her child, and Neil had been able to reduce the hours he spent in his job as a national account manager. He was now spending much more time with his family.

The growth had all been built on the foundation, the *bedrock*, put in place by adopting the simple 5 Levels of Formality list profiling system, and duplicating it through the team. More distributors experienced more immediate success and continued longer in the business all because they were coached on how to approach their contacts properly, from the start. Cases of *resistance*, *suspicion* and *ridicule* had reduced dramatically - almost to the point of being non-existent.

On reflection, the principles were so obvious and simple yet so easily overlooked in the excitement of getting a new team member started:

Before encouraging unskilled new distributors to approach their family and friends, set aside time to stop and think, and then teach them that the way to approach their contacts should be congruent

with how they usually interact with them, so as not to invite suspicion, resistance or ridicule.

Life was good. Of course, I was still good friends with Barney. He was still searching for the next shiny object that would make him his fortune, despite watching me rise through the company ranks. He always jokingly insisted on taking credit for my success, which I didn't mind. After all, it was he who had handed me the baton. What he always fails to mention is that it was me that had made the decision to take it and run with it.

So, you may be wondering, what happened to Dave, the painter and decorator that I was so desperate to prospect on the morning that my journey with Henry had begun? Did I ever get to share my business opportunity with him? Yes, it wasn't for him.

He was carrying a red balloon.

The End

So, now what?

We are firm believers in encouraging new distributors to take action as soon as possible.

That said, we <u>do not</u> believe that they should be encouraged to do so, fuelled only by *excitement*, like unskilled *lambs to the slaughter*, as so often happens. We all know how this usually ends.

It is our hope that, after reading this book and understanding the importance of acknowledging existing relationships, you now see the value of not only getting new distributors into action, but, more importantly, **pausing to consider those existing relationships** using the 5 Levels of Formality before making contact, so they can tailor an approach accordingly, dramatically increasing the chances of getting to share their business opportunity.

Remember:

> *"He or she who shows the most business presentations, wins." - Rosetta Little.*

Blog & Free Training Resources:

Visit www.5levelsofformality.com for FREE 5 Levels of Formality training resources.

Contact Danny & Paul: info@5levelsofformality.com

About The Authors

Danny Rich and Paul Robinson are partnered with a leading UK Network Marketing company and are up-coming, active distributors who have reached the top half of a percent of achievers within their organisation.

Born in industrial towns in the North of England, they met in 2008 and have become firm friends and business partners.

As well as enjoying building their respective businesses, they are also keen students of the Network Marketing profession and its underlying fundamentals and philosophies and are both dedicated to educating and equipping 'normal' distributors with the skills and mind-set required to build a successful business.

This book, their first, is a culmination of nearly two decades (between them) of books, audios, seminars and real life experiences based on the amazing world of Network Marketing.

Want to train the principles of the 5 Levels of Formality through your team?

The 5 Levels of Formality began life as a team training that Danny and Paul initially created for their own teams. Following positive feedback, they soon found themselves teaching to a wider audience, both on-stage at seminars and in a classroom setting. They now have a successful workshop, dedicated to teaching the principles set out in this book. If you are interested in finding out more, please email them for further information.

You can connect with them here:

info@5levelsofformality.com
www.5levelsofformality.com

Is there a book in you?

Are you harbouring a great book idea but are at a loss for how to bring it to life?

It's never been easier or more cost-effective than it is right now to get your book published - with the help of Scaredy Cat Publishing.

Visit www.scaredycatpublishing.co.uk
to see the comprehensive range of packages and let us help you get started making your own book a reality.

Printed in Great Britain
by Amazon